SCARY BUSINESS

SCARY BUSINESS

SCARY BUSINESS

Investing the Sudden Large Lump Sum

William S. Young, CFP®

MysteryCaper Press

Cover and illustrations by Katerina Vamvasaki

Editing services by Katherine Richards from *The Reading Panda*

ISBN-10: 0-9912324-9-6
EAN-13: 978-0-9912324-9-9

MysteryCaper Press
Columbia, Maryland

To my wife
Jeanne

For fifty years of loving support

Acknowledgments

The author would like to thank the folks at MysteryCaper Press for all their assistance and advice.

Table of Contents

Preface

You may notice an odd quality in the writing style of this book. There are numerous footnotes that just seem to state the obvious, such as "Past performance is not a guarantee of future results," or "You can lose money investing in stocks."

The reason for this is that I am still an active, licensed, registered representative of a broker dealer. Most financial writers, especially the well-known ones, are not securities licensed. They are able to say whatever they want with only their publishers looking over their shoulder. They can be witty, cleverly terse and express strong opinions without equivocating.

The licensed writer wants to do the same thing, of course, but it's a little like trying to tell a joke in Latin. It's not that it can't be done but it plays merry hell with the punch line. Licensed people have to say things in a "fair and balanced way" and make sure opinions are clearly labeled as such. Which is why people like Madman Cramer take care to resign their securities licenses before going into show business.

My hope is that you can overlook a few extra footnotes and disclaimers. I love this business too much to resign now. Besides, I'm barely in my seventies, a mere youth in the investment world. While major league shortstops are pretty much done by thirty-five, I've always felt that investment advisors start to peak in their mid-eighties. After all, investing doesn't require any heavy lifting or working out in the elements. It's a career that rewards wisdom, and that comes from experience.*

While Charlie Munger and Warren Buffett are great examples, I'm setting my sights on Phil Carret. He started a mutual fund in 1928 and was still giving investment advice to private clients up until a few months before he died…in 1998, at 101.

---

* *Experience being a code word for having made lots of stupid mistakes that you'll never make again.*

Introduction

    This is an intentionally small book on how to invest the **S**udden **L**arge **L**ump **S**um or "SLLS." If you picked it up as a do-it-yourself guide, toss it back on the shelf; you won't like it.

    The book is designed to help you accomplish your goals by working with a financial planner. There may be people who don't need any help investing a large sum, just as there may be a Bigfoot. But since the author hasn't met any of them in the last forty years—or encountered any yetis—we're going to assume they don't exist.

    When you look at the disastrous results of sports figures, actors and entertainers in handling large sums, you might think there are a few pitfalls—and you'd be right. Furthermore, just because you have money to invest doesn't mean you have to be interested in finance. Having money shouldn't be a chore.

    Essentially you pay a financial planner for three reasons:

1. They have training and experience in this area. Their guidance is potentially worth their fee because it may keep you from making mistakes that would cost a lot more.

2. They will do things for you that you would prefer not to spend the time and energy doing yourself.

3. About every five to six years, there's likely to be a bear market, and you may need the counsel of an

advisor who has seen all of this before, is totally familiar with your situation, and can help guide you through it.

The goal is not to turn you into an expert, but instead to help you find and work with someone who is. It's sort of like when you want to have your bathroom remodeled. For many people, the only home-improvement tool they know how to use is a checkbook. Most have no interest whatsoever in learning all the details; they just want a new shower. With that said, it might be very helpful to have some tips on problems that might come up and advice on working with the remodeling company.

That's the kind of book this is, except it's about investments.

Chapter One: The Sudden Large Lump Sum (SLLS)

There is a tide in the affairs of men,
Which, taken at the flood, leads on to fortune;
Omitted, all the voyage of their life
Is bound in shallows and in miseries.

—Shakespeare, *Julius Caesar*

"Large" is a relative term and putting a dollar figure on it is fraught with difficulty. Most people would consider $5 million a large sum...but not if they used to have a $100 million. Then it's a tiny figure that will barely provide subsistence-level income.

On the other hand, if you are living comfortably on $80,000, then $2 million is a colossal, life-changing sum.

For the purposes of this book, we will be defining "large" as an amount of money that you are unlikely to ever see again. A sum that, for you, is a financial game changer. Your future is tied to the use of this money...and there's no do-over if you get it wrong.

Typically, a sudden large lump sum (SLLS) comes from selling a piece of real estate or a business, or from inheriting. A significant subset of inheritance is when the death of a spouse leaves the surviving spouse with the financial reigns abruptly in their hands. While technically their net worth may not have changed, they now find themselves managing a large sum for the first time in decades, or ever. The effect is much the same; they now have to make money-management decisions.

Another source of large lump sums is from divorce settlements. This has in common with the death of a spouse that one takes on the financial responsibility at a time when emotions have probably already clouded the thinking process.

Finally, the most common source of a SLLS is retirement. This needs some explanation, since you may well be thinking that this is money you've been managing for years in your IRA or 401k. Nothing new here, so why should it be considered a "sudden large lump sum"?

There are two reasons. First, you are now in "no mulligan" territory, and that creates pressure. Much like walking along a foot-wide plank on the ground: no problem at all. But suspend that same plank between two ten-story buildings and try to stroll across. The tension can be so great you wobble about and fall.

The second reason is that you probably now need an **Income Portfolio**. This is a very different kettle of fish from the Growth Portfolio you are probably used to. An Income Portfolio has the goal of paying you an annual income stream *forever* and still growing enough to keep up with inflation. This puts very special demands on how the portfolio is constructed and managed. One year like 2008, without adequate preparation, can derail your whole plan.

This distinction is critical to investing the sudden large lump sum, because we are almost always dealing with an Income Portfolio. Clearly there will be cases where someone inherits or wins the lottery and will continue working because they love their job. But usually—once they stop and examine the situation—it is not a typical Growth Portfolio they want but rather an Income Portfolio *in waiting*, so to speak.

Even for those who have no income needs right now, the SLLS portfolio is virtually always an Income Portfolio. They want to continue working and already have the cash flow they need right now. But now that they have the SLLS, they want to be able to throw the switch at a moment's notice and start drawing income *if circumstances suddenly call for it*.

No matter how much you love your work, the situation can change. All kinds of things beyond your control can conspire to turn what used to be a pleasure to aggravation and drudgery. This is true for all occupations and endeavors.

We can't wait for that to happen and then throw the income switch on your portfolio and convert it overnight. Well, we *might* be able to do that, but it's not prudent to plan that way. Markets and stocks flow in cycles, so we want to think in three-to-five-year chunks of time. Growth Portfolios, by definition, are designed for a long time frame. You can afford to wait a few years if that great growth stock is in a periodic slump or tech stocks have gone out of favor. Time is on your side. But not when you suddenly want to make changes.

If you know when you are going to want an Income Portfolio, you should start building it five years beforehand. If you're going to retire at sixty-five, put your Income Portfolio together at age sixty, so it's there when you need it.

For the difference between a Growth Portfolio and an Income Portfolio to really sink in, we need to do a little math.[*] Most people hate math and charts, but sometimes nothing else will do to make the point clear. *Don't skip over this part!* Take a few minutes, and make sure these charts are clear and make sense to you. They're absolutely vital to understanding how an Income Portfolio differs from a Growth Portfolio.

Chart A shows a series of annual returns for $100,000 invested in a hypothetical **Growth Portfolio** over a twenty-five-year period.

Chart A

1993	**10%**	2006	**16%**
1994	**1%**	2007	**5%**
1995	**37%**	2008	**-37%**
1996	**23%**	2009	**26%**
1997	**33%**	2010	**15%**
1998	**29%**	2011	**2%**
1999	**21%**	2012	**16%**
2000	**-9%**	2013	**32%**
2001	**-12%**	2014	**14%**
2002	**-22%**	2015	**1%**
2003	**29%**	2016	**12%**
2004	**11%**	2017	**22%**
2005	**5%**		

The average annual return for this group of figures is 9%, and the ending account balance is $984,953.

---

[*] *This is a hypothetical example and is not representative of any specific situation. Your results will vary. The hypothetical rates of return used do not reflect the deduction of fees and charges inherent to investing.*

To demonstrate a point, let's rearrange the order the returns fell. On Chart B, let's pick out the three best years (1995, 1997 and 2013) and put them *first* as years one through three. Then take the 3 worst years (2001, 2002 and 2008) and arrange them as the *last* three years in our example.

Chart B

Year	Return	Balance
		$100,000
1	37%	$137,450
2	33%	$183,070
3	32%	$241,981
4	23%	$297,347
5	1%	$300,856
6	29%	$386,960
7	21%	$468,493
8	-9%	$426,047
9	1%	$431,373
10	12%	$482,361
11	29%	$619,834
12	11%	$686,405
13	5%	$719,146
14	16%	$831,620
15	5%	$876,445
16	22%	$1,066,370
17	26%	$1,348,852
18	15%	$1,549,966
19	2%	$1,580,500
20	16%	$1,830,535

21	10%	$2,011,575
22	14%	$2,283,339
23	-12%	$2,008,882
24	-22%	$1,563,914
25	-37%	$984,953

Note the ending value is still $984,953—a 9% average annual return.

Now let's take this same scenario but reverse the sequence of returns on Chart C. Now we start with the three bad years and end with three great years. **We've flip-flopped the sequence of returns.** Again, the average return is still 9%, and we have the same accumulation of $984,953.

Chart C

Year	Return	Balance
		$100,000
1	-37%	$62,980
2	-22%	$49,030
3	-12%	$43,137
4	14%	$48,964
5	10%	$53,807
6	16%	$62,319
7	2%	$63,547
8	15%	$73,022
9	26%	$92,365
10	22%	$112,381
11	5%	$118,438
12	16%	$136,962

13	5%	$143,495
14	11%	$158,906
15	29%	$204,194
16	12%	$228,330
17	1%	$231,184
18	-9%	$210,239
19	21%	$254,536
20	29%	$327,384
21	1%	$331,247
22	23%	$407,037
23	32%	$538,021
24	33%	$716,590
25	37%	$984,953

All of which proves 9% is 9% no matter how you scramble the annual numbers. Basic math—*but it can lead to a fatal complacency with an Income Portfolio!*

Let's do those numbers again but use our accumulated money in an Income Portfolio. Now we add taking a 5% withdrawal ($49,247) from our accumulated $984,953. Suddenly, 9% isn't 9% anymore. Look at Chart D.

Chart D

Year	Return	Balance
		$984,953
1	37%	$1,286,127
2	33%	$1,647,400
3	32%	$2,112,438
4	23%	$2,535,248

21

5	1%	$2,515,335
6	29%	$3,171,882
7	21%	$3,780,573
8	-9%	$3,393,267
9	1%	$3,385,820
10	12%	$3,730,955
11	29%	$4,730,994
12	11%	$5,184,566
13	5%	$5,380,273
14	16%	$6,164,798
15	5%	$6,445,178
16	22%	$7,781,929
17	26%	$9,781,068
18	15%	$11,182,835
19	2%	$11,352,919
20	16%	$13,091,912
21	10%	$14,332,584
22	14%	$16,213,015
23	-12%	$14,220,883
24	-22%	$11,032,618
25	-37%	$6,917,327

In this sequence of returns, **with the good years up front**, everything works like a dream. We average a 9% return and are only taking off 5% to live on, so the pot grows nicely. Your portfolio grows to a wonderful $6,930,530 over the next twenty-five years despite all the income ($1,231,175) you've taken. Perfect.

Now—drumroll here—turn to Chart E, the same annual returns but in reverse order, with the bad years first.

They still should add up to 9% because the sequence of returns doesn't matter…right?

Very wrong.

Chart E

Year	Return	Balance
		$984,953
1	-37%	$589,307
2	-22%	$420,436
3	-12%	$326,572
4	14%	$314,791
5	10%	$291,805
6	16%	$280,930
7	2%	$236,247
8	15%	$214,881
9	26%	$209,509
10	22%	$194,990
11	5%	$153,598
12	16%	$120,671
13	5%	$74,830
14	11%	$28,330
15	29%	--
16	12%	--
17	1%	--
18	-9%	--
19	21%	--
20	29%	--
21	1%	--
22	23%	--

23	32%	--
24	33%	--
25	37%	--

With an unfortunate *sequence of returns*, the Income Portfolio is crushed. The effect of withdrawing 5% makes an enormous difference, and the money is all gone by year 15!*

> ***There is a way of dealing with this sequence-of-returns problem, and we'll cover it in chapter 4.***

This shines a light on the four-letter word that's at the core of investing the sudden large lump sum: **RISK**. Chances are the potential investor is exclusively focused on market risk—what will happen if the stock market collapses? The media and internet make it clear that the apocalypse is due to set in with unusual severity any day, so this is perhaps not surprising.

But the very nature of the large-lump-sum investment is that the time frame we're dealing with is at least the balance of someone's lifetime and probably has multigenerational considerations. Therefore, a long-run view mandates thinking about all risks, not just CNN's frothy focus on where the market is going next week.

This is a hypothetical example and is not representative of any specific situation. Your results will vary. The hypothetical rates of return used do not reflect the deduction of fees and charges inherent to investing.

There are five classic types of risk, and each one has the potential to destroy a portfolio.

(1) Market risk is the one that everyone is aware of. The core component that is often overlooked is the time frame. Market risk is substantial over five years. But twenty years? How much weight do you want to assign to market risk over that time period? Empirical evidence would suggest much less than most people think.

(2) Purchasing-Power risk (or inflation risk, if you prefer) is a much larger risk than market risk over twenty-year periods. Rising prices were not much of a concern during the Depression era, for example, but by 1948 it took $1.40 to buy what cost a dollar in 1928. In a high-inflation period, such as 1972–1992, the cost of living can more than triple. Clearly when thinking of risk over long periods, purchasing power has to be taken into account as a major concern.

(3) Interest-Rate risk. The academic definition here focuses on interest rates causing the value of bonds to decline in a rising interest period. When you buy a corporate bond, for example, and interest rates rise, your bond declines in market value to reflect that lower interest earning. The holder of the bond is going to get less in interest payments each year than they could otherwise get on new bonds, so that has to be reflected in the market price of the old bond. The longer the maturity, the greater the interest rate risk. If the bond has eighteen years to go before it matures, you're going to get less money each year for eighteen years. If the bond only has two years to maturity, the interest rate risk is less because it's only going to affect you for a short time.

This risk also affects bank certificates of deposit, but most people don't think about that because their bank statements still show the same dollar value. Banks are not required to "mark to the market" the way bonds are, because CDs are not security products. Let's say you own a $100,000 five-year certificate of deposit at your local bank, and it is paying 3% interest. A year after you buy it, new CDs from that bank are now paying 5%, let's say. Your original 3% CD doesn't change in value on your bank statement—*but you are still suffering a loss.* The remaining four years of interest payments will be 2% shy of what the newer CD is paying, or -$8,000 in total.[*]

During times when interest rates are higher, there is the additional element of risk with rates falling and therefore making less income available. This was a major factor for people living off CDs paying 8% or more in the 1980s. When rates went down in the 1990s, their retirement income began to shrink. So, interest-rate risk can be a factor whether rates rise or fall.

(4) Financial risk. This is the risk that a company will fail and no longer be able to meet its obligations. In short, they might go out of business or declare bankruptcy. This is perhaps the easiest risk to deal with as you simply need to diversify.[†] (The Earl of Grantham from *Downton Abbey* discovered this the hard way in season 3.)

(5) Political risk is the danger that the government will seize an asset or business, make adverse legislative rulings, declare a product illegal or in some other manner harm a company or industry. There can be a tendency to dismiss this

---

[*] *This example does not deal with canceling the CD and paying whatever the penalty for early withdrawal may be on the CD.*

[†] *There is no guarantee that a diversified portfolio will enhance overall returns or outperform a non-diversified portfolio. Diversification does not protect against market risk.*

one as something for other countries to worry about. Yes, the United States was foolish once with Prohibition, but now surely it is only South American dictators who nationalize industries and turn their economies to mush. But in this age of class-action lawsuits and political manifestos, political risk should always be part of the equation. As with financial risk, diversification is one strategy to deal with political risk.

Risk is a multiheaded monster we have to deal with. By breaking it down this way, we can construct a plan, which is the subject of a future chapter.

Chapter Two: Selecting a Financial Planner

Before we get into planning, let's talk about why you should consider using a financial planner. In the introduction, we mentioned that there are essentially three reasons to use professional help. Let's focus on that first reason for a moment.

They have training and experience in this area. Their guidance is potentially worth their fee because it may keep you from making mistakes that would cost a lot more.

Unfortunately, for some people, these are fighting words. Men, especially, don't like to be told they don't know how to handle their money. They'll freely admit that they don't understand chess, quantum physics or classical music. But don't tell them they don't know how to drive, find their way without a map or invest money. It gets their male hackles up.

Oddly enough, there is a common female objection as well. Telling an intelligent, savvy woman that she needs help investing her money can sometimes come off as chauvinistic and trigger resentment.

The fundamental problem, for both genders, may stem from the popular myth that investing is easy to master and any smart person can follow a few guidelines and do fine. No one gets their back up, for example, if they're told defusing a bomb is tricky.

"Here, let me have a go at it; I've read several articles on defusing bombs and even saw a PBS special once."

Not so much. We automatically understand we should leave defusing bombs to the experienced expert. Even though we only need to snip the blue wire…or was it the red one?

But when it comes to investing, there's a whole industry of magazines, newsletters, books and television shows telling you it's easy and doesn't need any special training or experience. Sadly, even more harm is often done by well-meaning friends, relatives, neighbors, golf buddies and people you work with.

These are the people who have drunk the financial Kool-Aid somewhere along the line and now want to spread the gospel. These people are especially dangerous because they really don't know that they don't know and are therefore very sincere when giving bad advice. This is also where it's easy to be misled by the cognitive bias known as the "Halo Effect"

The Halo Effect is when someone who is successful in one area is given credit for expertise in a completely different, unrelated field. Dr. Jones is a highly respected brain surgeon and is therefore given credit for his financial advice, even though the two fields are utterly unrelated. Generally, when we like and admire someone, we tend to automatically give their opinions high marks without actually thinking through why they would be knowledgeable in a particular area.

The most common way the Halo Effect comes into the picture is with wealthy people. Those who appear to have plenty of money are assumed to be wise with investments. The fact that they got their wealth by choosing the right parents or by throwing a tremendous fastball is rarely thought through. Likewise, they may be burning through capital with terrible investments, and that wouldn't be apparent.

The big problem with bad financial advice is that, unlike bomb defusing, you can *think* you know what you are doing for years. Investing and financial-planning errors sometimes take a long time to show up and can be devastating when they do.

This is especially true when the stock market has been up for several years in a row, like it was in the late 1990s. In such an environment, it's very easy to confuse a bull market with investment savvy. Poor investment strategy, failure to diversify, lack of an adequate cash reserve and other foibles are all concealed by rising stock prices.

When a bear market does roll around, the pattern most of the amateur investors follow has a depressing similarity. They fret, worry, lose sleep and eventually sell out and put what's left of their portfolios in the bank, thus sealing their losses with no chance of recovery. It's human nature not to want to take responsibility for our own mistakes, so the final phase is, of course, blaming "those greedy Wall Street shysters" and never buying stocks again.

In investing, a little knowledge can truly be a dangerous thing. The older we get, the more we usually come to appreciate the adage that there is no such thing as a free lunch. A neighbor's advice may not come with a fee, but that doesn't mean there is no cost.

So, consider working with a financial planner! Now for the bad news.

Financial planners are pretty much like cops, carpenters, doctors, teachers, accountants, personal trainers, cooks and every other occupation you can think of. Ten percent or so are probably very good at what they do. Another 10% are moderately competent, and it goes downhill from there. You might think this is not a scientific assessment, and it's not. But it does seem that every occupation has a mix of competency and integrity in it, and financial planners are no exception. The goal here is for you to select someone from the top 20% to work with.

Let's start with credentials.

The Investment Advisor Representative

Being an "Investment Advisor Representative" may not mean as much as you think. It sounds impressive, but, in fact, it's quite easy to become one. Being an Investment Advisor Representative is a license more than a credential. (A RIA—a Registered Investment Advisory—is a firm; an IAR works for an RIA.) Having no financial background at all, one can take a weeklong cram course, pass a modest exam and poof!—you're an IAR. More importantly, if someone is an IAR and not otherwise licensed with a broker dealer, they may have less supervision going on than you might think.

Back in the '90s, FINRA (it was called the NASD back then) pulled off a brilliant coup. They didn't have the manpower, budget or expertise to supervise all the RIAs that were springing up. So, they essentially said that if someone was an IAR, *and also licensed with a broker dealer*, then the broker dealer must supervise and be responsible for their RIA activity. This brought most IARs into the supervisory fold so that someone was watching over what they were doing.

Of course, some IARs promptly dropped their securities licenses, telling their clients that they had opted out of that nasty commission business and were now "fee only."

However, the fact remains that having a securities license adds an extra layer of supervision with the broker dealer. Therefore, it may be better to stick with advisors who have a broker dealer affiliation. ***They can still work with you on a fee-only basis,*** but now you have an investment firm standing behind them in case there is a problem. You also have the FINRA regulatory body supervising, watching and inspecting to help protect your interest.

There are three credentials that are well known for financial planning: Certified Financial Planner (CFP®), Chartered Financial Consultant (ChFC) and Certified Financial Advisor (CFA).

Other impressive-sounding titles you may run across are likely to be something from a credentials-for-profit internet company, where you pay $350, take a multiple-choice exam and have your credentials within a week. (The better broker dealer firms usually prohibit their representatives from using those misleading titles.)

CERTIFIED FINANCIAL PLANNER™

The CFP® designation is widely recognized as the standard for financial planning. A CERTIFIED FINANCIAL PLANNER™ professional must have a minimum of three years of experience in the business, be sponsored by a financial firm and pass a six-hour comprehensive exam. The code of conduct for CFP® professionals puts the clients' interests first in all cases and requires commitment to a fiduciary standard in all their actions.

This "fiduciary standard" is a big deal. Stockbrokers (technically "Registered Representatives") have the obligation to make sure an investment fits within a broad category of investment objectives, such as "Growth" or "Growth & Income," for example. Beyond that, everything relevant about the investment needs to be disclosed. This typically means having you sign a paper saying you've read and understand the 180-page prospectus they gave you five minutes ago. (Of course, you didn't and don't, but that's neither here nor there.)

But if they are acting in a *fiduciary* capacity, it's a whole different story. Never mind that you, as the investor, love, understand and want to make this investment—you actually read the prospectus, let's say. Doesn't mean diddly. The fiduciary is held to a higher standard. The fact that you, as the investor, thought you understood the risk is irrelevant. The issue with a fiduciary is that, based on *their* training and experience, did *they* know—or should have known—that the risk was not appropriate for your situation?

It's a bit like skydiving. When someone goes splat, the skydiving instructor can't get away with saying: "Hey, they wanted to jump out of the plane." The issues are: Were they properly prepared, was the equipment in good order, were the weather conditions appropriate to jump that day? In other words, was this an accident that could have been foreseen based on having reasonable knowledge and education about skydiving?

That's what you get with a CFP®. They have a strong background in finance, and everything they do is pledged to the fiduciary standard. Which doesn't mean none of them are stupid or crooked, but you may have better odds here. (Full disclosure, the author has been a CFP® since 1985 and is biased.)

Chartered Financial Consultant

Those who have a ChFC designation have also taken extensive exams on financial subjects. One thing to consider with the Chartered Financial Consultant designation is that many, if not most, of the holders work in the life insurance area. Which doesn't necessarily mean they don't do a good job of giving financial-planning advice. But typically, the bulk of their income probably comes from insurance commissions, which may color their objectivity. The companies they work for may well have a minimum production standards for life insurance sales, which further tilts them towards recommending life insurance products over other products, in some cases.

This is a classic **Incentive Bias.** Countless studies have shown that people with a vested interest in something will tend to guide you in the direction of their interest. Many times, they are unaware themselves of how the incentive bias is clouding their thinking and genuinely think they are doing the right thing. In short, don't ask a barber if you need a haircut.

Certified Financial Advisor

The CFA designation comes from a very tough investment exam, and, again, applicants have to be sponsored by an investment firm before they can even sit for the test. The people who have this designation are very conversant with how investments work. However, the designation does not confer or represent any financial-planning knowledge. Often, CFA holders work for trust departments and mutual fund companies. Normally they are not giving advice to individual investors. If you want to know how an inverse straddle works, they are the people to ask. But if you want to know if you can afford to retire in six years, their advice may not necessarily be any better than your butcher's.

So, if you're considering working with a CFP®, the first step would be to find one with whom you're comfortable working to be your guide. You can get a list of CFP® professionals in your area by going to

www.letsmakeaplan.org

You probably want to interview three or more as personality has a lot to do with how comfortable you'll be working with someone. (See the list of questions you may want to ask in the appendix.)

A final point on credentials. What you want is someone who is honest, knowledgeable and experienced. No designation assures this, so don't rule someone out just because they are not a CFP®. But if you're on the fence between two advisors, then giving the nod to the CFP® probably makes sense.*

By the way, it's not the author's choice to keep putting the little "®" every time he says "CFP." The Financial Planning Board insists that it be repeated every time. Likewise, they don't want anyone to say "Certified Financial Planner" in the normal way one would. You have to say "CERTIFIED FINANCIAL PLANNER™ professional." Non-CFP® writers usually ignore all of this. But since the author is a CERTIFIED FINANCIAL PLANNING professional, he has to follow these

For anyone you're considering engaging, take a moment and visit **http://brokercheck.finra.org**. At this regulatory website, you can confirm that the person is licensed, what year they got licensed and if there has been any history of complaints or disclosable events. (Someone who is only an IAR and has no broker dealer connection won't be listed, which is another reason not to use them.)

When someone you know refers you to a planner, take a moment and give a little thought to how much weight you want to give to their opinion. Have they worked with this planner a long time? Can they tell you if the planner responds to email and phone calls promptly? Above all, *any talk about great investment returns* is the weakest referral point and far less important than if they think this planner is honest and easy to work with.

A great investment record is mostly about when funds were invested and will ebb and flow with the economy and market conditions. The old Hollywood quip applies here: "Whether your movie has a happy ending or not depends on where you decide to cut the film."

It's much the same with investment results, especially when you are looking at short (three-to-five-year) periods. If money was put to work in early March 2009, for example, your advisor probably looked brilliant over the next few years. (March 9, 2009, was the market low for the recession of 2008.) But this has little to do with the advisor's investment plan and everything to do with lucky timing. Most importantly, those conditions can't be ordered up again at will.

---

rules. They might not put a hit out on him if he flouts them, but why take the chance?

How quickly a planner answers phone messages and emails, however, is very much in the planner's control. Whether you feel rushed during an annual review has a lot to do with how the planner views your importance. When something goes wrong or there is a mistake made, does the planner stand behind you? These are the important clues a referral from a friend can help with, not investment results.

FEES

Typically, a financial planner will charge an asset-management fee based on the amount of money in your portfolio. Most are in the range of 1%, with perhaps a bit more on smaller accounts, and some discount once you go north of $2 million. Many planners also charge a flat fee in addition for putting the initial plan together.

Warren Buffett has famously said:

Price is what you pay; value is what you get. *The price is never an issue unless the value is in question.*

The trouble is, you may not be able to see the value for years, but the price is on your quarterly statement. Vanguard Funds did a study in September 2016 to determine how much value a planner typically brings to the planning process. Their conclusion was that it was about 3% a year. However, they were quick to point out that this 3% was an average and typically the benefit of working with a planner was "bunched." So, you may see little value that you can measure for some periods and then realize a lot of value over some particular incident or time period.[*]

---

[*] *Vanguard Advisor's Alpha, 2016, The Vanguard Group.*

What you should definitely ***not*** expect is for your financial planner to pick investments that will outperform (what you could have done yourself, what some index did or what your neighbors and golfing partners claim they did). He or she very well ***might*** outperform, especially over a full market cycle, *but that's not why you hire a financial planner.*

You hire the planner to help you work up a *written financial plan* that has a reasonable possibility of accomplishing your goals and then **keep you on track.** That involves risk management, which is a much harder thing to measure than a return percentage.

We'll be discussing this in more detail in the next chapter.

Chapter Three: The Financial Plan

No wind is favorable if you know not to what port you're sailing.

—Seneca

Seneca had it right. Another spin on this quote is: "Which is better, a pickup truck or a Corvette?" The answer is pretty clear if you know you're going to be hauling gravel. It's the same with constructing an investment portfolio. You first have to know what you're trying to accomplish, and that's what the financial plan is for.

Step number one is simply to gather up all of your information in one handy place. Who are the members of your family? How much money do you have? What other assets do you have? What are your income needs? What income will you have from other sources? What's your house worth, and how much do you owe on it? How long do you plan on living in it? Who's depending on you for income? What types of insurance do you have? What's your tax bracket now and down the road? Do you have any favorite charities? Who do you care about most in this world? What kind of legacy would you like to leave?

These answers need to be formulated into a written financial plan. The act of writing clarifies the objectives. The old saw that an oral contract isn't worth the paper it's written on applies here. If it's not written down, it's not a plan, it's just a conversation. It's only armed with this information that the right investment portfolio can be constructed.

One of the tasks that is frequently overlooked or passed over too quickly is taking a detailed and careful look at your expenses. Even though you may be running a healthy surplus right now, we still need to do this. This is the core of what your portfolio is funding. We need to look at what rising cost will do to this number over the balance of your lifetime—probably thirty years or more.

Most people hate this part of the plan. The idea of "budgeting" is repugnant to many and triggers—probably subconsciously—issues of someone else (parents?) telling you what you "should" be doing with your money. Shifting the way in which you think about it can sometimes work miracles.

The first step is reaffirming that you're the boss. **You can spend your money any damn way you please.** But how can you do that if you don't even know where it's going? That's the issue. Once you know that, you can make decisions on where to allocate it. Even if you're Bill Gates, there is still only so much money, and decisions have to be made.

For Bill and Melinda Gates, it's about their charitable foundation. Despite all of their resources, they can't support every worthwhile charity. When money goes to one deserving cause, it's not available to help five others whose needs are equally important. Life is about making tough decisions. Take a hard look at where the money is going. More on this after a brief digression.

How much income can you expect from your SLLS? For income, most financial planners will recommend a withdrawal rate on your portfolio of between 3.5% to 5%. While opinions vary on which is the right percent, virtually all qualified advisors agree that anything over 5% is begging for trouble. Let's take 4% as a compromise number.

Does your lump sum allow you to retire now, or does it need to grow for a few more years?

It's very easy to overestimate the income value of a large sum if you don't have a working model to test it on in your financial plan.

If you're currently earning $80,000 a year, a million dollars may seem colossal and surely the end of all of your financial concerns. But in terms of lifetime income, it's only going to produce 4% or $40,000. So, don't give up your day job.

> **What you don't want to do is follow Walter Matthau's example in *A New Leaf*. Anyone who has an SLLS to invest should watch at least a five-minute clip of this movie to see the scene where his trustee/lawyer tries to explain what "capital" is. Very funny and highlights the downside of overspending because you feel rich. Go to Google and type: "A New Leaf movie no capital"—that will bring up the scene on YouTube.**

Work through the financial plan to see how this new income, combined with social security and any other sources of income, will work. To do this, you need to know how much money you need and then see how it would likely fare over a thirty-year test period.

Now, back to budgeting for a moment to see how each element of the financial plan fits together. In most cases, there is some adjustment necessary between income and expenses. We frequently have to either increase income or decrease expenses to make everything work. Your choice— but here's the important point—*they're not the same thing*.

A dollar of expense money saved is worth the whole dollar. A dollar more in income isn't a dollar. You've got to pay tax on it, so it's probably only worth seventy cents or so. That makes lowering expenses—without giving up anything important to your happiness—so beneficial.

Imagine if an eccentric financial planner took out a thick stack of 430 crisp, new hundred-dollar bills and set it on the table and made the following offer to you. You can have this $43,000 if, next weekend, you set aside two hours and go over your credit card statements and bank accounts for the last twelve months and make a list of where the money is going. Give the planner the list and the stack of hundreds is yours! Good deal? Is it worth two hours of your time?

My guess is everyone would snap up this offer in a heartbeat and actually enjoy putting the list together since they were being so well paid for it. Well, this deal is on the table for almost all of us. Here's the point:

"What is $43,000 more in your portfolio worth to you?"

Let's do the math. We said we were going to take a 4% withdrawal from our portfolio for income. $43,000 @ 4% =

$1,720. Less income tax at an assumed rate of 30%, and you have $1,204 of annual spendable income—let's call it $100 a month. So, find $100 a month from your list that is an unnecessary expense, and it's the same as having an extra $43,000 in your portfolio!

Is budgeting still boring? How many things are you spending money on every month that are unnecessary or bring little pleasure? Food that you lug home from the store, let rot for a week and then put out in the trash? Gym memberships when you haven't worked out in months? Cable channels where you watch three movies a year? Dinner out when you could have had something from the microwave and enjoyed it more? It's a long, long list.

But worth the effort. Even if you've hated budgeting all your life, you may find this approach changes your outlook. For many people, it gets around the psychological blocks that have crept in over the years. You might even find you enjoy it!

Another aspect of the financial plan is tax management. If you've previously—before the SLLS event—been living from your earnings, you now have an opportunity to really manage your taxes, probably for the first time in your working life. With a salary, or income you take from owning a business, there is very little you can really do (legally) to avoid income tax. But when your income comes from an investment pool, new options are available.

If you have a portfolio consisting of both qualified accounts (IRA, 401(k), 403(b), etc.) and taxable investments, you have opportunities for tax management. Let's look at the following simplistic example:

$1,000,000	**Taxable Investments**
$1,000,000	**Regular IRA Account**
$2,000,000	**Total**

Using 4% for income, this portfolio will produce $80,000 to live on, along with your other income sources. But each of these buckets has different tax treatment, and that's where the opportunity arises.

Prior to age seventy, you don't have to take withdrawals from your regular IRA. So, suppose you're sixty-two and instead of taking any funds out of the IRA, you increase the withdrawal on the taxable account by the amount you might have taken. By taking $80,000 or 8% all from the taxable account, your tax bill will be substantially lower.

When you pull money out of your taxable account there is no tax unless there's a profit. From a tax standpoint, you're just taking your own money back. Much like having a bank account with $10,000 in it. You go in and withdraw $5,000—obviously no tax on that. You only pay tax on the interest earned. Drawing down principal is non-taxable.

There's no harm done to your portfolio if you draw down extra money from your taxable account if, at the same time, you are able to *earn an equivalent amount in your IRA*. You're just delaying taxes.

Now, of course, the catch is that you can't do this indefinitely. Eventually you'll run out of money in the spend-down account and then have to tap the IRA funds to live on. More likely you'll hit age seventy long before then and the jig will be up, but it's a great strategy while it lasts.

That's only one tax angle, and there are many others. Life insurance, variable and fixed annuities and Roth IRAs all have different tax treatment and potentially can be used to your advantage with proper planning. Each of these areas have to be explored in your plan to see how they can best be used in a tax-advantageous way.[*]

Do you support any charities? With proper charitable planning, you can maximize the benefit to your cause and perhaps save a bundle in taxes. If you have charitable intent, be sure to read chapter 8 on this subject.

Closely linked to charitable planning is legacy planning. What would you like to happen when you shuffle off? It calls for some careful thinking and can significantly affect how you arrange your portfolio. Chapter 10 covers the key points.

Finally, one of the best financial-planning tips the author ever came across, had nothing to do with finance. He got it from a grizzled, old bush pilot named Walter.

When I was young, I took flying lessons every Saturday. My regular instructor was a friendly, easy going guy who liked to explain all the details. He'd gone over with me several times how if your engine failed (single-engine plane) you could keep the speed down to about fifty miles per hour and set it down in a field somewhere, so it was a very safe aircraft.

One day, I showed up for my lesson and they told me my regular instructor had to be out of town so Walter was filling in for him. I wasn't happy about it—he looked cranky and unfriendly, but I didn't want to miss a lesson. As I went through my preflight checklist, he also proved to be taciturn in

---

[*] *Note that financial advisors are frequently not CPAs and you should consult your own tax advisor/accountant for tax advice before implementing any tax strategy.*

the extreme. By the time I took off, I think he had said a total of three words. ("Let's get'r up.")

As we flew along, I kept up a steady monologue on all I knew about flying so he wouldn't think I was just a beginner. He answered with his eyebrows or a wrinkle of his lip. In hindsight, I probably shouldn't have brought up my deep knowledge of how to handle an emergency landing.

We were at about ten thousand feet and he asked me where I'd land if I suddenly had engine trouble. I looked around and picked out a field. He reached over, shut the engine off and said, "Take her in."

I learned more in the next few minutes than I had in all my previous lessons. The key thing about a dead-stick landing is that you've got to get it right the first time—there is no do-over. As we got closer to the ground, I realized the field didn't look so peachy from five hundred feet. For one thing, there were power lines blocking my approach, and if those didn't do us in, the field itself was full of large rocks and far more trees than I had thought. Just as I was getting desperate, he turned the engine back on and said, "Get us out of here before you kill us both."

That was the last time I ever took a simplistic, ten-thousand-foot view of a future problem.

In financial planning, we're making plans with imperfect information about a host of things down the road. Don't fall into the trap of confusing what you *wish were true* with what a cool, clearheaded analysis would suggest.

Here are a few examples:

- *Assuming you will inherit*

- *Assuming your business partner has the same plans as you do*

- *Assuming your investment portfolio will earn an unrealistically high rate of return*

- *Assuming your job is secure and will be there as long as you want to work*

- *Assuming your health will allow you to work as long as you would like*

- *Assuming you and your spouse will love living out your retirement years in that little town where you vacationed so often*

These are just a quick sampling, but when you finish your financial plan, take a little time to focus on the details. Also work up some fallback positions in case everything doesn't go as planned. And stay away from power lines.

Now let's turn to how to go about setting up your investment portfolio.

But not to worry. You can live with the inevitable bear markets. The market being down only matters if you need to sell.

Let's stop for a minute and imagine that you had been born a trust-fund baby. Let's say your grandfather started a company that went public and developed into a first-rate, dividend-paying blue chip. When he died, he left a trust for his heirs and yours kicked in when you graduated from college. Your trust was held at a large, well-known bank and consisted of a portion of your grandfather's stock. Your initial income from the dividend was comfortable and almost every year went up, staying well ahead of inflation. In your case, this has been going on for almost forty years.

Then one day you just happen to catch an author—an expert on economics—being interviewed on CNN. This expert says the market is too high and bound to crash soon.

Do you suddenly become worried about your trust income? Do you call your trust officer in a panic? My guess would be no. You would be accustomed to the trust providing income for such a long time and also perhaps remember that your parents lived well off this same trust during their lifetime without any mishap.

So, no, another expert hawking his most recent book on TV is unlikely to cause panic.

Of course, you may not have had the foresight to be born with a trust fund. But now you can create your own with your SLLS—and it has the potential to be even better! Naturally you don't need to actually set up a trust, but what you do want to do is to think about your portfolio *as if it were a trust*, with a mission of providing income that can grow to keep up with inflation. The good news is you don't need to count on any one company, no matter how solid it is.

You may want to build a diversified portfolio of high-quality companies. These are the type of companies most people mean when they say "blue chip." So, imagine your portfolio is made up of well-financed, consistently profitable companies that have distinct advantages in their industries due to some sustainable competitive advantage. The goal is for the majority of these companies to be dividend paying and have shareholder-oriented management.

These types of stocks are what you might think of as "tennis balls." **All stocks drop from time to time—but tennis balls bounce.** * What you don't want in your portfolio are "eggs." Eggs are companies that have little cash reserve and depend upon the next round of financing to stay alive. They usually have a lot of debt and may not actually turn a profit for years. What they probably do have is a fascinating business plan with enormous potential. No matter how good their business plan is, *these are eggs*. They don't bounce well at all.

They may be great companies to own if you're thirty-five years old and have a Growth Portfolio you're adding money to every month. Many of today's highly thought of stocks were eggs in their early history. Such companies may have a great story and promise to be the next big thing—but stocks of that type have no place now in your Income Portfolio.

---

* *The phrase "tennis balls" is not an official term and is used as a shortcut by the author to describe stocks having certain characteristics. Such a description does not guarantee any future stock performance or assure that companies fitting this profile will always recover from a market downturn.*

Peter Lynch, the legendary Fidelity manager from the 1980s, was fond of saying he liked to find companies that "any idiot can run because sooner or later, one will." The mordant wit aside, what he was pointing out was that the management of any company might make a really bad decision on occasion.

Let's say, for example, some preeminent soft drink franchise was to announce that they were discontinuing their hallowed brand and replacing it with a new flavor. This might be viewed as a blunder of epic proportions. But companies with strong financials and tangible competitive advantages have the potential to work through the problem. However, if they weren't financially strong and—in the middle of the ensuing crisis—had to float a new junk-bond offering in order to meet expenses or go to their bank for a loan, they might not survive.

As a further risk-management measure, let's hire a whole team of talented, experienced people to watch over our portfolio. We do this by using active-management mutual funds and separately managed accounts (SMA) rather than index funds. The management team will then do such things as read each company's quarterly and annual SEC filings to keep abreast of what's going on. Also, we'll want these people to actually visit with the management of the company and interview their suppliers, customers and competitors to support what management is saying. (More on this in the next chapter.)

With this type of investment strategy, do you really need to worry about what "the market" is doing? The market is where you go to sell shares when you don't want them anymore or endeavor to buy more at an attractive price.

Benjamin Graham made this point eloquently in his classic book *The Intelligent Investor*. The stock market, he said, was a wonderful convenience. When you had shares that had reached their price potential you could sell them and when the market was down, you could pick up great companies at bargain prices. But if you were selling into a down market out of fear, then you were turning a useful convenience into a negative.[*]

Sixty years later, Graham's star pupil made this same point. At the 2009 Berkshire Hathaway annual meeting, Warren Buffett emphasized that the market was there to serve you and you should never sell out of panic or allow yourself to be put into a position where you have to sell because you need the money.[†]

Understand up front that you can't predict when the market is going to be down. So, whenever possible, plan on any large withdrawals well in advance so you can do them when share prices are up. Think in terms of a three-year lead time when you can.

Since the end of World War II, the market (after 1957, the S&P 500) has had a "correction" (a decline of 10% or more) on average about every fifteen months. About every five and a half years, there is a bear market (a 20% or more decline).[‡]

---

[*] *Graham, Benjamin,* The Intelligent Investor *(HarperCollins, 1949), p. 40.*

[†] *Pecaut & Wrenn,* University of Berkshire Hathaway, *p. 189*

[‡] *The S&P 500 Index is a capitalization weighted index of five hundred stocks designed to measure performance of the broad domestic economy through changes in the aggregate market value of five hundred stocks representing all major industries. The S&P 500 is an unmanaged index that cannot be invested into directly. Past performance is no guarantee of future results.*

So, again, do we really care what CNN tells us the cause is? Does it matter? We want to think of ourselves as partial owners in a collection of first-class businesses who live off our income as business owners. The market bouncing around for whatever reason is potentially only of concern to people with liquidity problems.

Consider Warren Buffett's situation back in 1987 when we had the greatest one-day decline ever—over 20%. The news media had a field day pointing out that he had lost an incredible $347 million!

But in reality, he didn't lose a dime. ***Because he didn't sell any shares.*** Seven months later, on May 27, his holdings had recovered to their former value. No loss, no problem.

Now you don't need to be Warren Buffett—you just have to act like him. Buffett didn't sell because he believed in his company and, most importantly, *he didn't need the money right then*. Which is how your funds can be set up with the proper cash reserve.

This starts with having the goal of a portfolio made up of high-quality, financially strong companies that have clearly defined competitive advantages in their industries and talented, experienced management teams committed to increasing shareholder value. (The idea here is to beat this point into the ground by constantly repeating it.)

Your financial planner can help you work towards this with carefully selected mutual funds that focus on these types of companies. You may also want to use a separately managed account. SMAs have much in common with mutual funds. They provide professional management and diversification, like mutual funds. But they have some important differences.

In a mutual fund, your money is comingled with all of the other investors in a giant pool. So, the actions of the other shareholders can have adverse effects on your holdings. For example, in a down market, clueless amateur investors blundering about tend to panic or try to time the market. (They mistakenly think someone is going to ring the all-clear bell when it's safe to go back in the water.) Unfortunately, their lemming-like behavior may hurt the other shareholders in the fund with them.

When the market has a temporary downturn, the fund manager has to sell shares to meet the shareholders' redemptions. First off, this may cause unwanted taxable gains. But also, when prices are low, you want your fund to be buying up great companies at bargain prices, not selling into a weak market.

The reverse also applies in a rising market. Your fund-management team does a terrific job and ends up on the cover of *Money* magazine as the brilliant, ten-star pick of the month. What happens? Money pours in and waters down future results as the management team struggles to find new companies to buy.

Both of these effects are difficult to measure with any precision, but they are headwinds the mutual fund manager has to deal with. We can potentially miss all of this with a separately managed account.

In the SMA account, no one except you can add funds to the pool or redeem shares. You have your own private account. And if taxes are an issue—and they usually are with sudden large lump sums—the SMA structure can help you manage tax issues more efficiently. You can control when you take losses and gains to some degree, which is not possible in a public mutual fund.

Every December you can instruct your advisor to accelerate gains or harvest tax losses in your account depending on what your tax situation looks like that year. You may not need to use this technique every year, but it can be very helpful when you need some tax planning.

As an aside, this same ability can be used for other reasons. You may already have a large position in some stock, so you don't want to buy more in this account. Or you may simply hate a certain company or even industry and want it left out of your portfolio. With an SMA, easy-peasy—but it can't be done with a mutual fund.

So, a combination of mutual funds and SMAs is often the building blocks of your portfolio. Mutual funds are also used because some desirable managers are only accessible that way. Also, mutual funds can be purchased in smaller blocks than SMAs, so a combination may work best.

The financial plan has laid out how much you'll need from the portfolio on an annual basis. The first thing we want to look at is how much of that will come from the dividend income the portfolio is currently generating, based on your *acquisition cost*. Let's make the assumption that the portfolio has an aggregate dividend yield of 3%, for example. We invested $2,000,000, so we can assume around $60,000 will come from dividends.

Dividends are not guaranteed, but they can, in practice, be fairly dependable when you are dealing with well-established companies. By having a pool of fifty to a hundred companies, your average annual dividend income may be smoothed out somewhat. Still, there will be some years where there will be a wave of dividend cuts and no amount of diversification will keep your income from dipping.

Let's look at a nice, long period, such as 1978 to 2018 to see how frequent these dividends cuts have been.[*] Over that forty-year period, widespread dividend cuts occurred twice, first in 1991 and then again in 2010. (Both dividend cuts were less than 10%.) In the other thirty-eight years, overall dividend income continued and stayed ahead of inflation for the period.[†] Past performance, of course, is no guarantee of similar results in the future.

As the book of Ecclesiastes reminds us, the race isn't always to the swift nor the battle to the strong. *But that's how you should bet them.* The odds generally favor the swift and the strong. The long-term history of blue-chip dividend payouts would suggest they may be a good source of an income stream for retirement.

Consider that the consumer price index tells us that you would need $181,985 in 2018 to buy all the things you could have gotten for $50,000 back in 1979. How would that have worked out with a fixed-rate investment?

In 1979, you may have been happy with your investment and received a high single-digit return that covered your expenses easily. But they don't have the ability to grow your principal, and future yields may be lower. That's the seductive thing about fixed investments. They

---

The author entered the securities business in 1978, so there is a prejudice for this period.

† These figures were gathered from mutual funds that focus on dividend-paying stocks and were active during this forty-year period.

make the front end of your retirement warm, fuzzy and comfortable…for a few years.

But you've brought a knife to a gun fight. Fixed-rate investments are excellent places to put funds when you have a short time horizon like three years. When we start looking at long time horizons—such as the rest of your life—your major risk is your purchasing power. It's hard to see how a fixed-rate investment can keep up with inflation. Similar fixed-rate investments in 2018 might be yielding a much smaller return. What did we say you needed…$181,985?

The back end of your retirement with fixed deposits might be anything but warm and comforting.

Your financial planner/investment advisor can no doubt show you some mutual funds and SMAs that focus on blue chips and have been around for many years so you can see how the above strategy has worked out in the past. Being a licensed professional, of course, he or she will remind you that past performance is no guarantee of future performance.

> *Never buy anything just because some author says it's a good idea. Work with your financial planner, and determine what is best for your situation.*

In setting up the portfolio, you'll want to consider adding a margin of safety by starting with two years' income in the bank. If you need $80,000 a year, for example, you would want to start with a bank deposit of $160,000 and have at least $2,000,000 left for the investment portfolio. ($2M at 4% = $80k.) This is one way to help deal with the sequence of returns problem we discussed in chapter 1.

This bank deposit should not be mixed or pooled with other savings. This is the money that is designed to protect your cash flow and is only used for income. For example, if the market goes down 20%, you could stop withdrawing from the investment portfolio and start drawing down the bank funds. This gives your investment portfolio the potential to better withstand the effect of bear markets.

Keep in mind that a down market isn't the same thing as an individual company's stock declining for some legitimate reason. Market declines (corrections and bear markets) generally do no lasting harm to good companies. In fact, strong companies might even take advantage of their weaker competitors during these periods and emerge with larger market shares. Market declines, per se, are not a concern.

But specific company problems are another matter. There aren't any stocks you can buy, put on the shelf and not worry about. Over the years there have been a lot of magazine articles and newsletters that gave lists of stocks you could "buy and forget." But if one went back and checked how that would have worked out over five, ten or even twenty years, it was usually a train wreck.

In August 2000, a major financial magazine had a story on stocks you could "buy and forget" that would let you "retire when ready." Six years later the portfolio was down by over 29% and the author of a new book on value investing used the article as a negative example, pointing out that one of the "buy-and-forget stocks" had already suspended trading, declared bankruptcy and was worth zero.[*]

There must be some psychological reason investors are drawn to these overly simple answers; wishful thinking perhaps. Which is why you might come across a writer or journalist advocating a "Coffee-Can Portfolio" approach to investing. This idiocy has been kicking around for years. The idea is to buy ten stocks you like and put the certificates in a coffee can and forget about them. Check in ten years to see how you're doing. Absolute lunacy.

What you should consider is actively managed mutual funds or SMAs. Someone has to read all the company quarterly and annual SEC filings. Someone has to meet and talk with your company's management team to stay abreast of any changes. Someone has to analyze events and changes within each stock sector to see how it affects your holdings. Someone has to monitor each holding's price movement in relation to its intrinsic value.

At least someone has to do all of this stuff if you want to stay abreast of what is going on at your companies. All of these functions, by the way, take way more time than most of us would ever be willing to give. (We do have lives, after all.)

Also, most investors don't have the training, practice and skills to avoid all the pitfalls that can come up with these activities. **Many of us may be delighted to pay someone else to take care of this for us.**

But wait, can't you just use index funds? Don't index funds beat all but a small percentage of active mangers?

---

[*] *Chris Browne,* The Little Book of Value Investing, *p.13.*

Well, it depends on how you phrase the question.

The studies that are often quoted and referenced to show the superiority of index funds over active management **assume you have no screening criteria at all for selecting your active managers**. Duh. The whole point of active management is to choose managers that have certain qualities you're looking for. Most financial planners will have several screens for selecting mutual funds.

The Capital Group did a study to examine how much using just two screens might improve investment results from active managers. The two screens were (1) being in the bottom quartile of funds for expenses, and (2) the mutual fund manager or team of managers had to have at least one million dollars of *their own money* invested in the fund they were managing.*

The report covered the twenty-year period of 1997 to 2016 and showed a clear advantage in investment results for the screened, active-management funds over their index rivals.†

If your financial planner believes in active fund management, they will no doubt be able to explain why they feel that way and provide an abundance of supporting information.

---

* *"A Screened Active Core Can Build Greater Wealth." This study is produced on American Fund's website (www.americanfunds.com) in several variations. The most recent (Jan 2019) is titled: "The Capital Advantage—Key Steps to Retirement."*

† *Ibid.*

Another reason for not using index funds or ETFs* to build your portfolio is that most of these indexes are constructed from data bases of potential stocks. No one yet has built a quantitative computer program that can determine if a company's management team is ethical, shareholder oriented, skilled at running their company and not planning to cut the dividend to finance some new project. Software programs are good at crunching numbers, not analyzing people.

Secondly, to some investment advisors, there are concerns with the way indexes are designed in terms of creating a truly durable portfolio. The most famous index is of course the S&P 500. This index was constructed to represent the US economy, and companies are included based on how "representative" they are of a particular industry. Note that the index committee is making no assurance that the companies in the index are profitable, have shareholder-oriented management or a sound business plan for the future.

It's also a "cap-weighted" structure, which means that the larger a company's capitalization (number of shares issued times the current stock price), the larger portion it is of the index. What this means is that as a stock price goes

---

An exchange-traded fund or "ETF" is a mutual fund that trades like a stock. With a regular mutual fund, redemptions are handled by the mutual fund company and you get the net asset value of your shares based on the 4 p.m. closing price on the day you submit your request. The ETF, on the other hand, can be traded any time of day, so you know the exact price, just as you would with an individual stock. ETFs may be based on an index, such as the S&P 500, or a range of other options such as a group of stocks that have some defining characteristics. So, if you wanted to buy a basket of high-dividend US stocks, for example, you could find several ETFs that do that. However, there are an increasing number of new ETFs coming to market that are actively managed. In this book, when the author refers to ETFs, the reference is to the non-active-management type or an index ETF.

up—and therefore gets more expensive—we buy more of it. Conversely as the price declines—and it becomes cheaper— we sell and own less of it. Does that really sound like the kind of strategy you want to bet your financial future on?

Now, most of the time, the S&P index is indeed going to represent the US economy and investors in mutual funds or ETFs that are modeled on it will probably do well. But consider the so-called "lost decade" of 2000 to 2010. For that ten-year period, the S&P **lost** 9%.

When that happens, the income investor may have to look to her cash reserve and dividend payments for income. Which is why we might seek to have a portfolio full of robust, financially healthy companies that are paying growing dividends. Stock market dips do not always correlate to reduced dividend pay outs. Well-financed blue-chip-type companies have historically continued to pay dividends, even in bear markets.

This was even true in the 1929 market crash—the mother of all bear markets. We all know the stock market crashed then, but few realize how deep and long that crash was. The market (Dow Jones Industrial Average) declined almost 85% at its lowest point and didn't recover to its 1929 high again until 1954.

Now that's a bear market! But even then, there were still companies that were well managed and well financed and continued paying and even increasing their dividends all through the Depression. As always, of course, past performance does not guarantee future results. This is merely to point out that financially strong companies with good business models certainly have the potential to continue paying their dividends during even a prolonged down market.

With all of this talk about dividends, a reader could easily slide into thinking that high dividends by themselves are the goal. Big mistake. If we can get high-dividend payouts with all our other criteria met, wonderful. But dividends alone do not fit in this strategy. The dividends have to be the result of the company meeting all the rest of our criteria. Which is why we don't just buy an ETF that buys high-dividend stocks.

It's the core fundamentals of the companies we want—and these will usually bring dividends with them—but not always. Also, all companies paying high dividends are not necessarily good investments. That high dividend may be propped up by something other than high earnings.

For example, managers of these companies are fully aware that their stock is held in ETFs and indexes focusing on high dividends. They also know what the ETF's listing criteria is in order to continue being part of the ETF holdings. The temptation to manipulate the dividend a bit to keep from being dumped can be strong. So, this is where active managers can add value.

There's an old engineering adage that applies to a lot of activities:

> *When you're up to your ass in alligators, it's often hard to remember you're there to drain the swamp.*

This frequently applies to building your investment portfolio. It's easy to get lost and slip into chasing the highest return. Remember, you don't *need* the best return; **you need the *lowest risk-adjusted* return that will do the job your financial plan calls for.**

The risk-management requirements of the Income Portfolio also rule out most of the exotic, unusual investments you may come across. Alternate types of investments that trade on an exchange or are part of a mutual fund may be a worthwhile part of your portfolio. However, non-liquid investments or investments that are not publicly traded may have unique risks.

The liquidity issue may not be a concern—you may well have plenty of other sources for that. The problem can arise if something unexpected happens and things start going south and you can't cut your losses and get out. You may be in for a long ride down with little to no control in an investment where the fundamentals are no longer good.

Even if the non-liquid investment has an option where you can submit your shares for sale every quarter, it might still be a problem. In the past, such offers have been withdrawn or suspended when too many investors headed for the door at the same time.

You may want to consider sticking to investments that trade on an established exchange and are 100% liquid every business day.

Before ending this chapter, we should say a few words about bonds. The role of bonds in your portfolio depends a lot on where interest rates are and where they are likely headed. Of course, there's the rub; no one really knows. For many years, the *Wall Street Journal* used to run a survey of economists and other gurus on where interest rates were going over the next six months. The experts rarely got even the direction right, to say nothing of the actual rate.

So, predicting interest rates is no better than trying to time the stock market. But there are some useful guidelines we can use for our own purposes. Since we want to set up an Income Portfolio to pay out 4–5% for living expenses, let's use that as a guideline. Whenever the Ten-Year Treasury Note matches what you are drawing down for income from a portfolio, they have some appeal. That way they contribute dividend income, which keeps the portfolio yield up. This helps balance out owning some stocks that pay no dividend. They can also be a good source of cash to buy stocks when the market takes a big dip.

The Ten-Year Treasury Note is the benchmark we might like to use as a reference, but in practice, we might use corporate bonds, municipal bonds, convertible bonds, foreign bonds or junk bonds as well. The maturities may also vary considerably from the Ten-Year Treasury. Analyzing which type—and even more importantly which *issuer*—of bonds to buy is something best left to the active-management experts.[*] For bond holdings in the portfolio therefore, hopefully your advisor will try to use a "strategic income fund" or other bond vehicle where the fund management has discretion to buy a variety of bond types and maturities.

Ideally, the bond holdings might be around 20% of the portfolio as a neutral position. That may seem low by traditional standards but you also have the two-year cash reserve. That's another 8–10% of the portfolio, bringing the

---

A bond manager once neatly summed up the issue, saying, "Bonds are both boring and complicated—a dangerous combination."

total non-stock portion to around 30%. Considering the rest of the portfolio is in high-quality, mostly dividend-paying stocks, this may be enough bonds, unless there are other extenuating circumstances. Again, your financial advisor, who is completely familiar with your position and cash needs, is the one to fine-tune these types of details.

It's best to ignore any rules of thumb you come across that match a suggested percent of bond holdings with an age bracket. Such things seem to be based on a flawed definition of risk. Going back to chapter 1, where we talked about the five different types of risk, your *time frame* tells you which risk is most important to protect against. If you are headed into a potential thirty-year retirement, your #1 risk is potentially inflation risk, not market risk. Stocks may help manage that risk, and there is no reason to load up on bonds just because you are seventy years old.

Another investment structure to discuss is annuities, but that's going to take a whole chapter down the road a bit.

Chapter Five: Why Active Management?

In the last chapter, we introduced the role of active managers and why they may be needed. There are planners who disagree with this approach. They prefer using index funds and exchange-traded funds, which are usually lower in cost. These planners may also believe the investment results will be better with indexes. (Apparently, they never read the screening study previously mentioned.) They also were probably not managing money for income clients during the "lost decade," when indexes didn't do so well.

Index funds and index-based ETFs can, of course, be a valid way to invest. This is especially true when you just want exposure to a certain area or theme for a limited time. But for the bulk of your portfolio, the theme of this book is that active management may be the best way to carry out a plan of only owning stocks that fit a certain profile. This costs a little more, which is what one would expect.

Keep in mind that the extra cost of active management doesn't go to your planner. It is purely to pay for the work the active management team does. The planner and his broker dealer get none of this. So, it's actually easier for the planner to recommend low-cost index funds than it is to defend the cost of active management. **The planner fee is identical regardless of which approach is being used.** What planner wouldn't love to move his clients' portfolios over to indexes and show how much money he was saving—if he was convinced it was the best thing for them?

When you think about all the things active managers do, you can see the potential for building a portfolio that focuses on certain key attributes. Companies such as these may potentially survive negative business developments, economic turmoil or bad management decisions better than their financially weaker rivals.

Using active management to build your portfolio needs to be a concept that resonates with you and you intuitively believe in. There aren't any studies on market risk that would be helpful in convincing anyone. For the purposes of any such study, "risk" would be defined as *market price movement*. Which is not the risk definition we care to focus on. Market price fluctuation doesn't necessarily mean the company's intrinsic value as a business has changed at all.

Frequently discussions around active management versus index investing tend to get mired down in what almost sounds like a political debate, with both sides trying to score points rather than examining the merits of each approach.

Instead, let's talk about what active managers actually do, so you can draw your own conclusions. A central concept with many active managers is to look at a potential stock purchase as if they were buying the whole business. You might think of this as the "Warren Buffett" approach, since he, in fact, does buy the whole company on occasion.

The first step is to establish what we'll call the "enterprise value."* What would a well-informed buyer pay for all of the outstanding shares of a particular business?

To come up with an informed estimate, the first thing that needs to be done is to separate out all of the GAAP (generally accepted accounting principles) numbers and replace them with real business numbers.

This termed is borrowed from an active manager who champions this approach.

This sounds confusing, so let's make sure we're all on the same page here. Let's suppose XYZ is a large, public manufacturing firm and owns a lot of real estate where they have their plants. They bought a particular building ten years ago for $40 million. Real estate has generally gone up in that area, and a conservative estimate of the building's value today is, say, $48 million, representing a 2% annual increase each year. So, you'd think the building would be carried on the books as a $48-million-dollar asset. But no, *for tax reasons*, they will actually be *depreciating* the value of this business asset under GAAP accounting rules. And this depreciated number is the one you see in the company's annual report. So, they might be showing the building as only worth $20 million, for example.

GAAP accounting also works in the other direction. Using perfectly legal accounting devices, there are numerous ways to make it look like you are making more money than you actually are in certain years. For example, contingent liabilities, such as retired-worker-health-care cost and other such things, can be carried on the books at a significantly smaller number than what is probably the case.

The active-management team will work through all of this and come up with what they believe the real, intrinsic value of a company is. This is what they believe a rational business person would probably be willing to pay if they were buying the whole company; the *Enterprise Value*. Then they divide this number by all the outstanding shares to see what the EV is per share. When you compare the EV to the current share price, you can see whether the company is trading at a premium or a discount to its intrinsic value.[*] That's step one.

---

[*] *There can be no assurance, of course, that the estimated value is correct or will ever be reflected in the actual trading price.*

Now they turn to income. All the same types of GAAP accounting versus reality have to be sorted out to figure what the company is really earning per share, which we'll call the *Owner Earnings.* So, if the EV (Enterprise Value) is $10 and Owner Earnings is $1, *and you can buy the stock for $10 or less,* you are getting a 10% or better earnings yield.[*] How does this compare with the risk-free yield you could get in a 90-day T-bill? In 1989, when you could get an 8% T-bill, this stock may not have looked too appealing. With a ninety-day T-bill paying 0.5%, it's a different story. That's step two.

Step three is to take a hard look at the company's management. Typically, this will be an in-person meeting to see where the company is headed and how management is assessing the business climate. What problems do they see, and what do they consider their company's unique, competitive advantage? Meetings with the company's main competitors, suppliers and customers will usually follow to determine how clearly management has analyzed their position in the industry.

From all of this, the active manager will decide whether they'd ever want to own this company and at what price.[†] Some active managers will charge less than half a percent to

---

[*] *This yield is a rough guideline for valuing a company and is not the same thing as a dividend yield. Owning such a stock will not provide you with income at this level. Stock ownership involves various risks and investors may lose money.*

[†] *This process that has just been described is an example of the type of procedure that some active managers use but will vary considerably from firm to firm. Your financial advisor can provide you with more precise information about specific investment managers you are considering using. All investment related decisions should be made by consulting a licensed professional and not made based upon the general concepts put forward in this book.*

do all of this (1% is a hundred basis points in investment jargon).

What you get thrown into the bargain is everything the management team has learned over their respective careers. When the author visited one active manager's office some years back, they had a board on the wall where they listed all their biggest mistakes over the years. This acted as a constant reminder of what can go wrong and what they *learned from the mistake*. That kind of thinking and humility has the potential to produce a great management team.

Mistakes and errors in judgment are always painful. But if the lesson is well learned, that's one less mistake that particular manager is likely to make in the future. The dictionary defines wisdom as "the quality of having experience, knowledge, and good judgment."

Another major element of active management is their research department. These are the people who follow certain industries and the key companies within those industries. At many active-management companies, this is an entry-level position where you have to pay your dues for a few years while you work your way up to portfolio manager. But at some firms, research is a career path all by itself.

At those firms, you may find analyst who have followed a particular industry for twenty years or more. Would you think this brings any special insight to investment decisions? One major active manager's research team has over two hundred analysts from fifty-two countries, who collectively speak forty languages. If you personally were making all of your own investment decisions, would you find the ability to ask these people questions about various companies and industries of any help? If you were trying to decide which of two companies in the same industry to buy, would it benefit you to talk to an analyst who had been following both companies for the last twenty years?

Now, the index crowd says, "Nah, none of that is necessary. Cost is all that matters, and we don't need any of that information to make decisions. Not worth the time and trouble."[*]

Perhaps. But the companies that pass such a screening process sound a lot like the "tennis balls" we discussed in chapter 4.

In comparing active management to indexes or ETF funds, another point is that if something happens with a company you own—a major contract is lost, a talented CEO dies, fraud or something like that is discovered—the active manager can sell the stock that day and perhaps minimize the damage. But the index funds and index-based ETF funds have to wait until their next scheduled rebalancing. That could be a few weeks or even longer, depending on when their next committee meeting is scheduled. Another potential plus for active management to take into consideration.

---

[*] *The author's discussion of active and passive investment strategies, as well as economic and market conditions, is for illustrative purposes only. There is no guarantee that these statements and opinions are correct. Equity markets are volatile and investors may lose money.* **Past performance is not a guarantee of future results.** *The author's opinions include forward-looking statements which can be identified by words such as "believe," "expect," "anticipate," or similar expressions. You should not place undue reliance on these forward-looking statements, which are current as of the date of writing but will not be updated unless there is a revised edition of this book in the future. The author and publisher would like to specifically adjure readers not to rely on this book as specific investment advice on any product or plan. Consult a licensed, qualified investment advisor before putting money into any investment approach discussed in this book.*

When you have selected a financial planner to work with, they will naturally have their own approach to setting up your portfolio. They will also have their own favorite fund groups they like to work with. Do be cautious, however, if your planner seems to primarily talk about past investment performance as the main reason for fund selection. **There should be solid reasons for using funds that have nothing to do with trailing returns.** Investment returns, by themselves, are potentially the worst possible way to select managers.

Investment results give you information about what has been happening over a specific period being measured. The shorter the measuring period, the less it is actually telling you. Three years, for example, basically lets you know what was low in price at the starting period or conversely what style or investment approach has been hot for the past few years. Health-care stocks or technology stocks may have been the investment theme of choice. Will that be the same over the next three years? Probably not. Do you particularly want managers who focus on those types of stocks?

Even longer periods of time, such as ten years' investment results, say less about the fund management than they do about market and economic conditions on the starting date. Perhaps, ten years ago, large well-established blue-chip companies were very much out of favor. Therefore, prices for those stocks would have been depressed at the starting date, making the current ten-year numbers look very good. Does this tell you much about the management? Again, it's mostly about the economic climate of the particular measuring period.

Ah, but surely when you look at twenty- or thirty-year periods, you can draw some conclusions about a fund manager's abilities. Not so much, actually. For one thing, even if the fund manager is still there, there have surely been other personnel changes that might be significant. Also, the fund may have been very tiny at the beginning and has now grown very large, which may affect future performance. And how much longer will that manager stay on if they have already been there for twenty or thirty years?

So don't chase returns or focus on past performance. What you want is a group of active managers that have an investment process that makes sense, is likely to be repeatable, and is well matched to your particular financial plan and goals.

Chapter Six: Dealing with a Bear Market

We all know what the word "cold" means. But did you ever notice how much differently you think about it when you're sitting around a comfortable room, say with a crackling fireplace? Try this experiment. When the weather outside is near or below thirty-two degrees, step outside without any coat or sweater. Stand around for a few minutes, then chat (or, if alone, just think) about how lucky you are to have a warm place to live in.

You'll almost certainly be more appreciative than when you were back by the fireplace. You can *feel* the cold now; it's not just a concept. Your emotions will be engaged.

That's how bear markets are. You can read about them and intellectually understand what's going on. But you're still sitting by the fireplace with a lamb's wool sweater. It isn't until you have a substantial amount of your net worth in stocks and have had the experience of opening your quarterly statement and seeing that you're now down 26% that you really understand a bear market.

Except you won't think, *Gosh, down 26%*. You'll convert it to dollars. On a $2,000,000 portfolio, that's $520,000. Chances are, before the SLLS, you had a lot less in the market, so the impact of down markets was less visceral.

Now the trouble begins in earnest. You start listening to television shows and reading the financial press. What emerges is that this is no ordinary bear market. This time *it's different*. Unlike previous bear markets, this one has a very clear cause, and the financial press is right on top of it. One thing they all agree on is that it's **going to get much, much worse. Be sure to tune in at eleven to find out why.** Is it getting cold in here?

This would probably be a good spot to pause and talk about journalists in general. The key thing to be clear on is that they are not in the business of educating you or anyone else. Their incentive bias is to get you to buy their magazine, newsletter or book or to watch their TV show. Education and truth have very little to do with it. Financial regulators require that licensed individuals make "fair and balanced" presentations and even regulate such things as the print size on their letterhead.

Not so for journalists; no one regulates them (nor should they), and they can present the facts in any twisted way they wish. A classic example of this is illustrated by two editions of the Baltimore newspaper that were one day apart. On Tuesday, April 5, 1994, the *Baltimore Sun*, reported a 42-point drop in the stock market on their front page. Of course, in journalese, stocks never decline—they **PLUMMET.** So, the front-page headline, in bold giant print, usually reserved for royal coronations or alien spaceship landings, read: **"Stocks Plummet to 6 Month-Low."** Keep in mind the market was down 42 points.

The **next day**, April 6th, the stock market was *up* **82 points.** If you had that day's *Baltimore Sun* in your hand, you might have to hunt a while on the front page to find the stock market news. Buried below another bad-news headline in bold print on rising mortgage rates, you'd find a postage-stamp-sized box in regular print saying, "Stocks Rise." This was the largest one-day gain in three years, but apparently *The Sun* felt it wasn't very newsworthy—since it was *good* news.

With all sincerity, could anyone look at those two pages and actually think the *Baltimore Sun* gave a fig about educating anyone or even reporting the news in a neutral fashion?

This isn't to pick on the *Baltimore Sun*. The *Wall Street Journal*, the *New York Times*, the *Washington Post*, the *Chicago Tribune* or any other newspaper are all guilty of similar things. **And we shouldn't blame them!** It's not their fault that bad news sells. Their incentive bias drives them to feature negative, and hopefully *frightening*, things to keep your attention.

The real fault, as Cassius pointed out to Brutus, is with us. Journalists are in business to sell advertising space, not educate us. We should not be expecting something else. How much education could they possibly provide anyway, in the typical short news article?

This is also true when we look at radio and television. They need to have something attention getting to say very quickly or you'll change the channel. This also applies to expert guests on the shows. You see, people who are cooperative and have good quotes get invited back and also get to be guests on other programs. This makes their sales departments happy.

It all boils down to incentive bias again. As Deep Throat told Woodward, "Follow the money." Highly rated TV shows make a lot of money. Being a guest on a highly rated show is generally viewed as a very positive thing if you have something to sell yourself (your book, newsletter or the mutual fund you work for perhaps).

Sourly telling your host that the subject is very complicated and can't be explained in a ninety-second sound bite isn't likely to get you invited back. Having positive, uplifting things to say about *anything* will probably get you labeled as a Pollyanna who's out of touch with current events—and not invited back.

In a nutshell, just as you shouldn't get your medical advice from the internet, don't get your financial advice from a journalist (on the internet or otherwise). Talk with your financial planner. They have the right incentive bias.

What does your fee-based CFP® want? They want you to be happy with their service, stay a client for the rest of your life and recommend them to your friends, associates and especially your adult children. They want your account to grow as much and as fast as is prudently possible without undue risk. ***All of these things make them the most money.*** So, their incentive bias encourages them to treat you great and try their best to grow your account. When your account doubles, their fee doubles.

When the market heads south, your planner suffers too. Their fee goes down with your account balance. The last thing in the world they want is for your account to suffer a disastrous loss through some ill-conceived investment. If planners thought there was a safe way to side-step a down market, they'd be all for it. The beauty of the financial-planning incentive bias is that it is perfectly aligned with your own goals and desires.

When the market is down, talk with your financial planner. Listen to what they advise. If you don't have confidence in their advice or trust them, by all means get a new planner. But be wary of this step. Has something changed with the planner, or have you discovered something you didn't know about them before? *Or are you just panicking because your account is down half a million dollars?*

82

If the latter, be careful. In bear markets, it's not uncommon for some unprincipled investment people to promote their alleged market-timing ability. They may say they foresaw the coming drop and all of their clients were safely in Treasury bonds or a money market where they will sit until this all bottoms out. You may even be referred to someone like this by one of their happy clients. Such claims are very difficult to verify.

Do you know how horseracing touts work? The tout visits bars and such and gives someone a free tip on the next day's race. He tells them to bet a bundle on the #3 horse. It's a sure thing. Then he finishes his beer and finds another gambler. Bet it all on horse #4, he assures him, it's in the bag. And so on until he has covered all seven horses in the race with as many people as possible.

The day after the race he visits with all the people he told the correct selection. They'll be happy to see him and pay more attention now to what he has to say. So, he gives a tip on another race. By pure math, by the end of a few races he'll have someone he's told three straight winners to.

This guy is very impressed. After a few drinks, the tout reluctantly reveals that his cousin, brother or former cellmate works at the track and knows when the fix is on. He must be legit, he predicted three straight winners! From this point, the con has many variations depending on the financial resources of the mark.

This is merely to say, don't get too impressed with the supposed market timing of your neighbor's planner. If something sounds too good to be true, it usually is. As long as we've had stock markets, there have always been timing and other magical schemes floating about. They may even have worked for a while…until they didn't.

Also, market timing isn't without its own risk. According to one study, if you invested $10,000 in 1990, it would have grown to $51,354 over the next fifteen years. But if you missed the best ten days, you only had $31,994. If you missed a whole month (out of the 180 months), you were down to $15,730. If you missed the best fifty days, you ended up with $9,030.[*]

Market timing is like alchemy; it can't work almost by definition. Many scientists in the past labored away to discover a way to turn lead into gold. Leaving aside that there isn't any practical way to do this, there is a bigger problem. Suppose you *could* turn lead into gold? Do you really think you'd always be the only one who figured it out? Soon gold would be as common as, well, lead and worth very little.

It's the same with market timing. You have to understand that every transaction in the market requires two parties: the buyer and the seller. So, if you discover the magic sign that the market is going to go down, how long will this be exclusive information that only you know? And once the word is out, where is the buyer half of the trade going to come from?

Most of the investors in the past who have actually made a lot of money in the stock market—Phil Carret, Sir John Templeton, the Davis family, Peter Lynch, Warren Buffett—all tend to scorn market timing. Their advice is to avoid any variation of it. Simply ride out bear markets.

---

[*] *Chris Browne,* The Little Book of Value Investing, *p. 128*

Bear Markets are necessary and healthy. Shelby Cullom Davis, a well-known investor after World War II, liked to say: "You make most of your money in a bear market…it just doesn't feel like it at the time."[*]

Many mutual fund managers have "Buy" boards of some sort. This is where they list all of the companies they'd like to own but were just too expensive at the current trading price. Next to each name is the price they'd like to pay for it. When a bear market comes along, it's like ringing the dinner bell.

While the press is telling you to panic, mutual fund managers are more likely to be loading up on great companies at low prices. This is why many great mutual fund companies tend to have wonderful bounces when the market recovers.

Someone—it may have been either Templeton or Buffett—quipped that a bear market is when "stocks were returned to their rightful owners." (The amateurs who had bought companies at high prices sell out to the professionals at low prices.) Don't join them! Remember that bear markets can be a good thing in the long run.

Even when the market isn't in a tailspin, there is plenty of market movement for the new SLLS investor to deal with. Journalists, financial regulators, academics and other amateurs all call these price swings "risk." The godfather of all securities analysts, the man who mentored Warren Buffett when he was at Columbia University, disagrees. Benjamin Graham was emphatic in *The Intelligent Investor* that this was

---

[*] *"The Wisdom of Great Investors," Davis Distributors, p. 9.*

not risk. This was simply market *volatility,* and the two were not the same thing.[*]

Market volatility means the price moves around within a range. The wider the range, the more volatile the stock or mutual fund is said to be. The buzzword here is "standard deviation." Such movements do not necessarily or even usually reflect any fundamental changes at the company level to warrant any price swing. But academics and regulators have locked on to this statistic and labeled it "risk," feeling no doubt that they have a finer understanding of the matter than Benjamin Graham did.

This is mentioned because, as an investor, you are constantly bombarded with talk about risk. It is important to have a clear understanding of what different people mean by the word, because it's not uniformly the same. Within the scope of this book, when we say "risk" we refer to an irrevocable loss of money—not a temporary decline due to market conditions. That's volatility, and it only becomes a true loss if you do something irrational, like sell.

When a stock declines in price due to some negative development at the company itself that is a different matter. Now we are talking about real risk, not volatility. A new assessment needs to be done in light of the new development to determine whether the stock should be sold or not. Again, this is what you pay active managers to do for you.[†]

As was stated earlier, bear markets typically come along every five and a half years or so. But mini-bears (or "Teddy

---

[*] *Graham, Benjamin,* The Intelligent Investor *(HarperCollins, 1949), p. 73.*

[†] *Which does not guarantee that the active-management team will be successful or correct. Losses on individual stocks occur in actively managed portfolios despite their best efforts to avoid this.*

Bears," if you prefer) happen all the time, and they can upset new investors almost as much. This is where, if you measure on a different time period than the calendar year, you get different results.

For example, a recent study covered the sixty-nine-year period from 1946 to 2014. Of those sixty-nine years, 71% (forty-nine years) had positive returns on a calendar-year basis. But here is the rub. **Virtually all of those positive years had negative intrayear periods.** So, if you measured from, say, March 3 to October 30, you may get a negative number.

Why would you be doing this? How about your SLLS was originally invested on March 3, and seven months later you're looking at your October statement that just came in the mail. You've heard several news reports that the market is up 10% this year. So why are you down? Your investments must be bad!

It's easy to miss that when the media says the market is up this year, they naturally mean for people who were invested on January 1. The stock market tends to move in short spurts. So, over a three-week period in January, let's say, the market shoots up. Later investors will have missed that and also paid more for their shares after the rise that just took place. So, their numbers won't look as good at first. But these differences have the opportunity to even out fairly quickly, and after a few years may mean very little. But if you're new to investing and just put your SLLS into a portfolio, it can be unsettling.

Anytime you're making a comparison with your portfolio results, make sure you're working with the same dates. Equally important, make sure you're comparing apples to apples.

Your portfolio, which may have an allocation of 30% in non-US stocks, might not move in sync with the US market. Chances are you have some bonds in your portfolio. They're certainly not going to move with stocks; they march to a different drummer as well. The whole idea of comparing your results to a market index is ill-conceived if you have a solid financial plan.

Your financial plan is custom designed to show how you can accomplish your goals and has a return target that will make all of that work. If your portfolio is well set up and is likely to meet your return goal over a full market cycle, then you don't need to fret over how you're doing versus this or that index.

Chapter Seven: Annuities

Back in the late nineteenth century, annuities were a common way to handle retirement. You gave the insurance company a sum of money, and they would pay you an income stream for the rest of your life. The amount depended on how old you were and what the interest rate was at the time.

The snag was that once the deal was in place, you could no longer access your funds. Of course, that wasn't always a bad thing. You couldn't make a bad investment, lose all your money, and end up on the street. Likewise, you couldn't loan or give money to needy family members and ruin your comfortable retirement. As long as the insurance company was sound, you didn't have to worry about market collapses, business failures or turbulent economies. The big downside was that when you died, the insurance company kept the money, so you didn't leave any legacy.*

This type of *fixed annuity* is not very popular these days but it can still be an appropriate fit in some circumstances. Back in early 2009, for example, before interest rates collapsed to record lows, a fixed annuity might have had strong appeal to investors who fit a certain profile.

For instance, if you were an eight-nine-year-old who was in good health, had no heirs or legacy concerns and was primarily interested in maximizing income, a fixed annuity

---

* *There were usually some stipulations that gave some protection. If you died early, someone else might have been named to receive the money for the balance of ten years or some other time period.*

with a solid insurance company at that time may have paid out a double-digit return (mostly due to the annuitant's age).[*] In those circumstances, this product might be ideal. Admittedly, situations such as that are not common, but they are far from unheard of. Every financial product has good and bad features and when used for the right job works well.

Fixed annuities are also offered as "deferred annuities," where you give the money to the insurance company and they pay an annual interest rate, much like a bank. You have the option of "annuitizing" your contract whenever you wish and taking a monthly income for life. Or you can simply cancel your policy and take your money back. (Normally there is a surrender charge if you cancel within some period, typically between four and seven years.)

There are also tax considerations. The interest you earn is not taxed as long as you keep it in the contract, but the IRS stipulates that you must not surrender the contract until you are $59\frac{1}{2}$, the same as if it were an IRA deposit. If you do, in addition to the taxable interest, there is a 10% penalty imposed. Like an IRA, you can also transfer the money over to another insurance company without triggering any tax, since you're not taking "constructive receipt" of the funds. (This is called a 1035 exchange.)

If you do annuitize the contract and start taking an annual (or monthly) income, there are some further tax advantages. The IRS recognizes that some of that monthly payment from the insurance company would, in effect, be a return of part your own principal. So, they designed an annuity table that determines how much of each payment is interest—and taxable—and how much is just a return of your own money and not taxable.

In 2009, the author wrote such an annuity on one of his clients who fits this profile.

(In the event you use an annuity with IRA funds, all the annuity tax rules go out the window and the IRA rules override them. IRA accounts are all taxed the same, regardless of what investment is funding the IRA.)

Once fixed annuities started offering competitive interest rates without requiring that you ever annuitize, they became a different product. Their market was no longer limited to people who were looking for a secure monthly retirement check. Essentially, they were competing with bank certificates of deposit and corporate and government bonds. As IRA accounts grew in size and popularity, this became a hot market. Banks even jumped on the bandwagon and started selling annuities themselves through their branch offices.

The key to understanding these new fixed annuities is to think of them as if they were, in fact, corporate bonds. The credit worthiness and claims-paying ability of the insurance company are important. Because of the nature of insurance companies, they rarely fail outright. Even when they do declare bankruptcy, they're typically taken over by some other insurance company who will make good on their obligations to annuity holders.

However, this isn't pleasant to have to deal with. You may get all your money back, but it can be an annoying procedure and may well take years and interfere with your retirement or other plans. You may also get your initial investment back but not at the promised interest rate. All in all, it's best to be cautious when one company is offering substantially higher interest payments than all of their competitors. Pay attention to their claims-paying rating from companies like AM Best, Fitch, Moody's, Weiss and Standard & Poor's.

Also watch out for the contract details. Many times, high first-year interest rates are just to get you hooked in. If the contract has a five-year surrender clause, they then have four years to pay lower rates and recover the bonus they paid out in the first year, for example.

With an SLLS to deal with, the more likely annuity for you to come across is a *variable* annuity. Essentially this type of contract was originally a portfolio of variable subaccounts with an annuity wrapper to shelter you from income tax during the growth period. These were the types of annuities that grew in popularity from the '70s on. In the early '90s, they introduced a "living-benefit rider" that became popular. There were (and still are) many variations, but in essence the rider offered a lifetime-guaranteed payout without "annuitizing" the contract. So, you were able to access your money if you wanted and even more importantly, you could leave the full account value to your beneficiary.

These contracts exploded from about 1995 to 2009, offering baby boomers who were approaching retirement a wealth of desirable features. There was full tax shelter until you started taking income. The living-benefit riders were guaranteed to increase in value every year by 5, 6 or even 7%.

So, in those key growth years coming up to retirement, you didn't have any zero or negative growth years despite what the stock market did. When you started to draw income it was locked in, usually for both you and your spouse for the rest of your lives. And remember, these accounts were invested in variable sub-accounts, so you might have still earned potentially high returns some years. Typically, if the contract value had increased during the year, it would

92

lock in this new higher value as a new guarantee, which would increase your subsequent guaranteed payouts. What's not to like, right?

Well, there is always something; no financial product covers all of the bases perfectly. Let's start with the guaranteed benefit rider. The first thing that is commonly overlooked is where the payout is coming from. Every dollar that is sent to you from the guarantee is deducted from your account value. While this makes perfect sense, we often miss what this really means.

The insurance company isn't at risk for a penny until the account goes to zero. Typically, you can't (or don't want to) start drawing income until you are age sixty-five. If the guaranteed payout is higher than the account value, it's still usually a long time before the insurance company has to add any of its own money to the pot.

Let's suppose your account actually earns only 4% but the insurance company is forced to pay you 5% because of the guarantee. It could still be years before the account value runs to zero, so they're not on the hook for anything yet. Which means the living-benefit rider's main value is mostly psychological—it lets you sleep at night.

But don't minimize this feature. Many investors in 2008 stayed invested because they had this guarantee. So, the rider benefit may have been "only" psychological, but the returns they got in 2009 by staying invested were certainly tangible and real.

But while the insurance company's risk is minimal, they still collect a generous fee for providing this guarantee, somewhere between .40 and 1.78%, depending on the company and the rider.* Many companies, by the way, charge the rider fee on the amount of their guarantee, not your shrinking account base. The fee never goes down despite your account balance shrinking—therefore, the fee becomes an increasing drain on your account value.

Can't the investment account earn a healthy 7–8% and everything works peachy? Yes, it can. But the odds are against it. Virtually all variable annuities restrict the investment choices in some way if there is a living-benefit rider. This could be anything from requiring at least 30% be in bonds to having the right to arbitrarily move 75% of your portfolio over into bonds if they wish.

There is nothing wrong with bonds, *per se*, as we discussed in chapter 4. But in a low interest-rate environment, they lose some of their appeal. The real problem is that bonds may work very well for the insurance companies' goal—preserving principal as long as possible. Whereas your goal is to have the portfolio grow, so it can provide a rising income stream and keep up with inflation.

Therefore, it's unlikely that you will be earning anything like stock market returns with a variable annuity—and that's not the insurance company's concern. They don't have any skin in the game until you're at a pretty advanced age, and by then they will have racked up a lot of fees to help cover any liability they may end up with.

So far, we've only been talking about the rider fees. The annuity structure itself has what they call M&E cost—meaning mortality and expense charges, which are typically

---

* *These fees are representative of ten to fifteen variable-annuity contracts the author examined. There is no guarantee of completeness in this statement of fees, as there are many other variable-annuity contracts the author did not analyze.*

1.65% or so.[*] There are also fees internal to the investment subaccounts.

With all the expenses and rider fees, you're typically paying 2–3% in expenses. This makes it unlikely that the investments will be so good they'll be able to overcome this cost every year, and these expenses may become a drag on the performance. But there are other things that potentially make it even more unlikely that your investment account will grow.

Let's take a five-year period leading up to your retirement when you are not drawing anything off yet and the market is having a rough spot. We'll assume your investment is $100,000, just as an example. Let's say that a well-diversified investment portfolio only earns an average of 4.26% for this period. This amount is further reduced by all the annuity fees that have to be paid out of this account. Your net growth could easily be only 1% for the period. But your living-benefit rider provides (for example) a whopping 6% net compounding guaranteed return since you're not taking income yet.

So, your living-benefit rider at a net 6% has increased over the five years to $133,823. You can now start to draw 5% of that amount for the rest of your life. This type of low-return period makes the living-benefit rider look pretty good. You not only earned 6% net when the market struggled, but you paid no tax on the growth and can now start to draw off $6,691 forever.

_____

One percent of this expense is usually paid out to the registered representative, so, in that way, it might be considered no different than a 1% advisory fee in terms of an expense. The 1.65% figure was also taken from the previously mentioned survey of ten to fifteen variable-annuity contracts and does not represent a comprehensive study.

Almost everyone would be happy with this deal and feel good about their future retirement. But there is a potential risk here; it's just hard to see at this point. This $6,691 needs to grow to keep up with a likely rising cost of living. The only way it can grow is if the actual investment account is greater than the current guarantee on the contract anniversary. How likely is that to happen in this case?

Well, we're starting in the hole. In this example, your actual investment account only has around $112,281 in it, but it has to support an annual withdrawal of $6,691, which means we are drawing down at a 6% rate on an account that is already struggling to support high expenses. As was mentioned in an earlier chapter, most experts advise that withdrawal rates be between 3.5 and 5% *to allow for adequate growth*. So, the odds are heavily stacked against ever getting an increase.

Understand what that means. Over the last twenty years (as of June 2018), we have had a fairly benign inflation rate of 2.17% (according to the US CPI Index). But even with this mild inflation, in twenty years the purchasing power of your $6,691 will have gone down to $3,594—almost half. Taking a fixed income into a rising-cost environment can be hazardous.*

---

* This is a hypothetical example and is not representative of any specific situation. Your results will vary. Economic forecasts set forth may not develop as predicted.

Variable annuities may be suitable for long-term investing, such as retirement investing. Withdrawals prior to age 59½ may be subject to tax penalties and surrender charges may apply. Variable annuities are subject to market risk and may lose value.

Riders are additional guarantee options that are available to an annuity-contract holder. While some riders are part of an existing contract, many others may carry additional fees, charges and restrictions, and the policy holder should review their

It would not be wise to put your whole SLLS portfolio in a living-benefit rider and assume retirement is on autopilot.

But a variable annuity (VA) with such a rider may still work for part of your portfolio. The good thing about such products is that they may provide a steady, dependable cash stream, which can be very useful during the first ten years of retirement, while your other more traditional stock investments have an opportunity to grow. This is especially true during periods where other traditional cash-stream sources, such as bonds or bank CDs, have very low payouts.

Another plus for annuities is tax shelter if we are not talking about IRAs or other already-sheltered accounts. For taxable portfolios, gains often come in large chunks, and that can mean a big tax bill even with capital-gains rates. But in an annuity, you only pay tax on what you take, which can help you manage your taxes. When your VA earns more than you took to spend you can leave the surplus in the VA, where it will have the potential to keep growing without any current tax drain.

Here you have to balance this tax shelter against the different tax rates that apply. The annuity forfeits capital-gains treatment on stocks and everything is ordinary income. This can be modeled in your financial plan to see which appears to work best for your circumstances. You and your planner may also want to bring your CPA into the loop to get their opinion on what works best for you.

The final annuity product you might run across is an *indexed* annuity. These are a hybrid product in that they combine features of both fixed annuities and variable

contract carefully before purchasing. Guarantees are based on the claims-paying ability of the issuing insurance company.

97

annuities. Essentially, they work like a fixed annuity but instead of an interest rate, they link their return to some index, such as the S&P 500.

It might be a five-year contract for example that offers up to a 7% return depending on how well the S&P 500 does during the period. There is usually a "participation rate" that says your return will be 70% of the S&P return, but— and here's the big appeal—you can't lose money. If the market is down, the worst that can happen is you don't earn anything. Wow, a product that gives you 70% of the stock market return (S&P 500) but you can't lose anything!

Sounds appealing, but these things have some challenges. Generally, they are very difficult to analyze. The people who sell these products do not need any securities training or licensing; only an insurance license is required. Not technically being a securities product, the disclosures may not be as detailed or clear.

So, when these products promise some participation rate like 70% they look appealing, especially since you can't lose anything if the market tanks. But your expectation of participating in a rising market may not be feasible.

What isn't clear in much of the product literature is that the participation rate is typically broken down by *days* over the measuring period and capped at some daily max. So, the market could have a great day and be up 4%—but you would only get some tiny gain, like a tenth of a percent, due to the daily maximum. An analysis of these products versus the actual stock market performance for the same period frequently showed that very few of them actually paid the expected participation rate due to daily maximums.[*]

---

[*] *While the author has examined perhaps a dozen contracts over the years, this is far from any kind of exhaustive study.*

Back in the 1990s, when these products started to show up, some paid high first-year commissions. With that kind of up-front expense, it's hard to see how the investor benefits.

Some financial planners now say that these companies have changed and cleaned up their acts over the last ten years. Or new companies have now entered the business and offer a more reasonable product catering to risk-sensitive investors. Maybe. But proceed with extreme caution, and pay careful attention to what the sales commission is and how long any surrender penalty lasts.

To recap this chapter, annuities may be a useful part of your portfolio as long as you understand the downsides and have a clear feel for how they fit into your plan. Fixed annuities may only work well in specialized situations or when interest rates are high. For indexed annuities, use extreme care and make sure you understand all the details.

Chapter Eight: Charitable Intent and Donor-Advised Funds

If you are one of those lucky people who have discovered the life-enhancing joy of helping others, or supporting a noble cause, then having a sudden large lump sum to invest may call for some extra planning. As was mentioned in chapter 3, the SLLS may allow you to manage your taxes for the first time ever.

However, that can have a downside for your charitable endeavors. If you have been a longtime member of your church/synagogue/mosque, or have a special cause you like to support, it is unlikely that you'll want to stop doing that just because you're not getting much of a tax deduction. Here's one way you may be able to still benefit.

Set up a donor-advised fund when you're still in a high bracket—the calendar year you received your SLLS, for example. Setup can be relatively easy and cost effective. These DAFs are usually sponsored by a mutual fund company, bank or other financial institution. Annual fees to the sponsor typically vary between .65% and 1.25%, depending on how much is in the fund. These costs are not paid by you directly but come out of the invested assets of the DAF.

Wherever you set yours up, it can function for you much like your own private foundation. But whereas the Bill and Melinda Gates Foundation operates in a fishbowl, you will have total privacy. Anyone with access to the internet can quickly look up how much money is in the Gates

Foundation, what they earned on it last year, and who they made grants to.

With the DAF structure, no one knows how much money you have or where you are distributing it. Your particular DAF doesn't need to file any reports or forms each year—that's all taken care of by the sponsor. While someone may be able to look into the DAF sponsor's assets as a whole, they can't see what your particular account has or does.

Another difference is that the Gates Foundation and all other private foundations *must* distribute at least 5% of their assets in grants each year. DAFs do not have this requirement. So, you can put $50,000 in your DAF, fully deduct the entire deposit in the year you put it in, and not make any grants to anyone if you don't want to for a very long time. *

This feature makes it useful for financial planning. It disconnects the tax benefit from the charitable benefit. **This is huge!** What are the odds that your church's roof blows off in the same year you are desperate for tax deductions because you just sold your business?

With a DAF, you can control the year you get the tax benefit and distribute funds to the charity in totally different years.[†] Now, of course, you could—and most people do—simply give extra money to your favorite charity when you are having a high tax year. But this has a significant downside—you've lost control.

---

* *Tax laws are, of course, subject to change in the future and there can be no guarantee that any future change will preserve this current rule.*

[†] *You get your deduction in the year you put the money into the DAF. When you subsequently make a grant to a qualifying charity, you don't get a second deduction, of course.*

You give $50,000 to your church because you need the deduction this year. Now suppose a month later, the pastor dies or leaves for some reason. Their replacement shows up and starts taking the church in a new direction—one you don't like at all, and they have your money to help their new program! Happens all the time. Or suppose you decide to move? The church can't give you back the money so you can support your new church in either of these cases. Same applies to your alma mater or any other charity.

Even more common is that some new charity comes to your attention—perhaps because some illness is contracted by a loved one. Suddenly you might very much regret that big donation you made a year or two before and wish it were available to help your new cause.

But with the DAF all of that can potentially be avoided. You get the deduction in the year you need it for tax purposes and maintain control of your funds. This can play out in some very interesting ways in your financial planning.

When people have charitable intent, it's part of their budget even when they retire. With a DAF, you could put money away prior to retirement, when you may be in a higher tax bracket, and get a tax deduction, and the funds have the potential to grow tax deferred. If the funds are later distributed to a 501(c)(3) charitable organization, you don't pay taxes.

You can therefore continue to make contributions to your favorite charities in retirement without dipping into your other income sources. This is similar to an IRA, where contributions are deductible and have the potential to grow tax deferred, but whereas IRA distributions are subject to ordinary income tax, money from a DAF isn't taxable when distributed to an eligible charity.

There are also some non-tax-related features of the DAF that can be very useful. For example, have you ever had a neighbor/friend/coworker approach you about giving to some charity they're collecting for? It can be awkward, because you have your own causes you are supporting and don't particularly want to contribute—especially any significant amount. But there are often social or business relationships to consider.

Your DAF can give you a classy way out that may even improve your status in the eyes of the one soliciting money without you writing a big check.

"Oh, Bob, I'd love to help, but our accountant has got Susan and me committed to doing everything charitable through our foundation now. I know the foundation's grant budget is all firmed up for this year. I'm so sorry."

Remember, your neighbor or whoever, probably felt awkward about approaching you for money to begin with, so this gives them a graceful way to move on as well. In some cases, you might not mind making a small donation but know that the amount of the donation is going to reflect this person's standing with you as well as your own. If so, a slight addition to the above will set this up perfectly.

"I'd like to help, though. If I leaned on the grant committee a bit, I could probably shake loose at least a token grant. Would something like $200 be worthwhile?"

If necessary, you can also add that the way the foundation works is that you can only *suggest* grants to the committee and can't make them yourself. This is, strictly speaking, absolutely true—there is no need to add that the committee is unlikely to refuse unless something is amiss with the charity itself.

A couple weeks later, a check in the amount of $250 arrives in the name of your foundation. (Note the extra $50 so they will know you really went to bat for them.) Chances are this will enhance your status more than a $1,000 donation would have, and everyone is happy.

Another handy feature is the ease of making donations and keeping your tax records simple. Instead of gathering up canceled checks, letters confirming the donation and so on at tax time, you simply have one letter from your DAF confirming any tax-deductible deposits you made in that year. All of the outgoing grants can be done online, and it's much simpler than writing and mailing a bunch of personal checks.

It's also nice to know that a quality check is always done by the DAF before they send out a new grant. This is designed to confirm that the charity is legit. Usually this isn't an issue, but where it does come up is when there's been some natural disaster like Hurricane Katrina. It's hard to know which organization to send money to and fraud does spring up in these situations. Your DAF will run a verification before dispersing any funds.

A final point on the non-tax-related benefits of a DAF revolves around those heartbreaking solicitation letters we all get. Think twice before sending them any money! The little girl with the sad face is unlikely to see a penny of your donation. Explaining the sordid world of charitable fundraising is outside the scope of this book so you'll have to take this as a given. The charity in question is most likely on a cash-cow campaign using a *for-profit* outside company to help them produce a list of potential donors.

As much as 100% of anything you send them will be used to pay the fundraiser or to cover the expense of resoliciting you for the next two years. Nothing or very little will go to help the avowed cause on the envelope. But if the letter has aroused your interest in the cause, do a little research and see if you want to support them.

Then send a donation from your DAF. This will disconnect the "you" who was on the original mailing list from the donation. All of the grant you send will go to actually helping the cause, since nothing is drained off as a solicitation expense. Charities don't waste their time soliciting DAFs since they know the actual grant instigator will never see the letter. (DAFs don't forward junk mail to you; it all goes straight to the shredder.)

You win by not being harassed by endless, annoying solicitations. The charity wins big-time by receiving funds with no connected fund-raising costs. And most importantly, the little girl on the envelope may actually get a warm bowl of soup as a result. It is always sad to see charitably minded people wasting money by sending out dozens of $25 checks every month in response to these letters.

The charity that sent you such a soliciting letter may be a good one, but that doesn't mean you have to follow the instructions in the letter. Use your DAF to help the charity in a much more efficient manner.[*]

---

[*] *This information is not intended to be a substitute for specific, individualized tax or legal advice. We suggest that you discuss your specific situation with a qualified tax or legal advisor.*

Chapter Nine: ESG Considerations

"ESG" stands for environmental, social and governance. This use to be called "SRI" investing, which stood for "socially responsible investing." But the buzz now is ESG, which conveniently lumps the three broadest "clean" categories under one umbrella. The idea is not to buy stock in companies that run afoul of these screens.

This approach might have a lot of appeal to you if you drive a hybrid or electric car, recycle, refuse to use chemicals on your lawn, loathe smoking, believe in the humane treatment of animals and think companies have certain moral obligations to their employees (things that all apply to the author).

But ESG investing may not be the most effective way of embracing these values.

When you refuse to buy a tobacco stock, for instance, that isn't directly hurting the company. Unless this is a new stock offering, the shares you buy are just from some other investor. The company doesn't get anything; they raised their money by selling stock a long time ago. Current shares are just moved around with different investors.

Of course, no company wants its stock to be unpopular and slump in price as a result, but you're not hurting them directly. Investors frequently think, *I'm not giving any of my money to a tobacco company so they can sell cancer.* A wonderful sentiment, but that's not what is happening.

Let's say you are rabidly against the sale of tobacco products. But you can't buy an ESG fund that avoids tobacco without picking up a dozen other banners at the same time. Most ESG funds also won't buy alcohol stocks, for example. Are you also anti wine and single malt? Same with gun companies. Our law-enforcement agencies have to buy weapons from someone, so unless you want our police to defend themselves by throwing rocks, it's hard to see why you should be against the companies that supply them with firearms. And so on.

Most ESG concerns are double-sided. We can't all drive a Tesla, so why try to punish those oil companies *that strive to be ecologically responsible* and provide a very essential product for the other 99% of the world? Those who are lucky enough to live in a developed nation frequently forget what life is like for millions of people living near the poverty level. Having a gas-powered motor scooter or access to low cost fuel to heat their homes makes quite a difference in their lives.

Furthermore, it's hard to see the logic behind not buying oil-company stocks but continuing to use oil-company products. If you're concerned about carbon emissions, surely it does more good to drive a hybrid or electric car, use solar power for your house and try to avoid petroleum-based products when an alternative is available. This is far more productive than not buying energy stocks.

How about women's rights? Not paying women equal pay for equal work is something any right-thinking person would strongly object to. But is it widely happening now? By who? Certainly not union companies. Not in any occupation that is based on commissions. Not in any government agency. Most large companies are acutely aware of how this would put a target on their backs and are highly unlikely to go down that road. This leaves us with a few small companies apparently run by morons. Is this something to base your investment decisions on?

You occasionally do hear about some large public company being sued under some equal-pay rule. But in many of these cases it smacks more of a political, public-relations shakedown than a real issue. Typically, some law firm would have statistics that showed *the average female employee* earned less than the average male employee—but not for the same work. Many other distinctions applied and were conveniently ignored in bringing the suit.

Working outside, for example, is not as pleasant as being in an office and may pay more. Work-related health risks are found disproportionately in male-dominated work. (Workers killed on the job are about 96% male.) So, lots of things result in uneven pay for various jobs besides gender discrimination.

A close relation to this theme is when ESG managers blackball a company because they don't have a high enough percentage of women on their board of directors or in key management positions. While this may be a concern, assigning quotas by gender is a heavy-handed solution that just changes the gender being discriminated against.

A good stock analyst would probably be quick to pass over a company if they knew or suspected that they had a policy of rejecting qualified women for top positions based on gender. That's simply bad management. But that decision should be made by a stock analyst, for investment reasons, not by some quixotic committee that has no skin in the game at all.

All of this boils down to the fact that the minute a mutual fund or other investment manager hangs out the ESG banner, they cede too much control to people who have a non-investment-related agenda. The ESG approach is a shifting target and new criteria is always being added.

Certainly, each mutual fund or SMA makes their own decisions as to what ESG concerns to use as a screen for stock selection. But when the United Nations, the Sierra Club or some other organization adds a new activity or company to their blacklist, the ESG investment funds are likely to knuckle under. If you want people to buy your ESG mutual fund, you have to toe the line.

When looking at ESG management firms or even just reviewing their literature, it is always clear that the ESG concerns override all the regular, fundamental stock-selection criteria. A company can have great potential and solid financials, but if they fail an ESG screen, they're out. Now some ESG companies do occasionally buy stock in an offending company with the idea of putting pressure on the board to modify their policies. This is an appealing idea, but typically we are talking about a few select positions, and the overwhelming majority of stocks selected still have to pass the ESG screen.

Many ESG managers—and the media—love to say that having an ESG criteria is actually just good investment selection and companies that don't pass their screen are bad investments anyway. So, you can feel good about your companies and still have the type of durable portfolio we want. But does that really hold true?

Sin stocks can have very respectable returns. Sometimes less virtuous companies perform better than their squeaky-clean counterparts for very long periods of time.

All of these ESG issues are more important if you are dealing with an SLLS Income Portfolio. If you are talking about a *Growth Portfolio*, that's another matter. If you want to buy ESG funds with a long time horizon and no income needs, that may be more appropriate. Companies that are attuned to ESG concerns may, in general, be more suitable in a Growth Portfolio.

But the purpose of this long rant is to urge you not to focus on ESG concerns in investing your SLLS *Income Portfolio*. Remember, you don't get any second chances here; you've got to get it right the first time. Don't shoot yourself in the foot by building on a weak foundation.

Yes, if your planner builds your portfolio based on the principles we talked about in chapter 5, you will potentially have a few companies mixed in that you don't like or at least aren't ideal. But you'll also have the type of portfolio that has been designed in an effort to weather the economic rough seas that will inevitably turn up.

(As mentioned in chapter 4, with SMA portfolios, you can remove companies that are particularly offensive to you. Try to limit this so as to not upset the investment mix too much.)

If you are the type of person that ESG considerations speak to, chances are that you may also have charitable intent. Until the perfect blend of ESG and investment considerations becomes available, perhaps you could simply focus on that. Let your portfolio be set up purely on investment principles with the idea of aiming to secure your finances. Then use your income to help the causes you believe in while you're living, and leave larger amounts to them in your legacy planning.

This approach worked well for Alfred Nobel—he made his money selling dynamite and armaments but is remembered today for the Peace Prize. When you look at how much Nobel money has flowed to charities since 1901, it's hard to conclude he would have done more good for the world by being a dairy farmer instead of a munitions salesman. Luckily, he didn't have to pass an ESG screen.[*]

* Investing involves risk, including possible loss of principal. No strategy assures success or protects against loss.

112

Chapter Ten: Legacy Planning

Legacy planning involves who you are going to leave things to and in what manner. We went over any charitable plans you might have in an earlier chapter. The legacy planning, of course, includes all of that and adds your individual bequests.

There are several reasons to go over this in your financial plan. The obvious first consideration is that none of us know when our estate will be settled. So, the best time to think and talk about this is when you're healthy and have a long future in front of you. The worst time is when a terminal illness has been diagnosed. That makes all the conversations and discussions that much harder for everyone. So, get this taken care of when you can be clearheaded and plan to live forever.

A word on whom you name as executor. You may think it's a great honor for your sibling, who lives six states away, to be selected, but it's more like a parting curse. There is lots of time-consuming, frustrating paperwork and it all gets worse at a distance. You may want to name the honored person as a co-executor along with the local law firm that drew up the will.

Yes, this will cost more. But it lets the attorney, who is trained and experienced in this area, handle all of the work. That money will be well spent to spare your spouse or some other loved one from having to deal with all of this. Yet they will still have input as the co-executor.

This also applies to any trusts you have set up in your will. Use a corporate trustee that has a "family advisor" position. Name your loved one as an advisor to the trust, not the trustee. That way they can keep the trustee informed about what would be appropriate or request specific distributions without having to get involved in any of the actual trust work. The corporate trustee can then be the bad guy when it's called for rather than the family member.

Legacy planning also involves thinking about which assets would work best to carry out your wishes. For example, consider an estate plan where a widow is leaving 10% of the estate to her church and the rest divided up among several more distant family members.

Among her other bequests, she has a $72,000 IRA account where she has two nephews listed as the beneficiaries. Her intent is for them to each get $36,000. But they aren't going to get that at all. IRAs have a sizable tax bill that has to be paid first. The nephews could set their inheritance up as a "beneficiary IRA," but then they still wouldn't have access to the money without paying the taxes. Also, they would be required to take an annual IRA distribution, and, if they forget, the penalty is a whopping 50%. Altogether, perhaps not the best arrangement.

What if you change the beneficiary on the IRA to the church? Churches are generally tax-exempt, in which case it would get the whole $72,000. The two nephews could each get $36,000 from some other assets. Many other assets have little quirks that make them better suited for certain purposes.

Life insurance, for example, has many unique qualities that can be helpful. For one thing, it normally pays out very quickly, typically in a couple of weeks at the most. (Policies that are less than two years old may take longer, as they are still subject to contestation.) Estates are normally much slower, and it could easily be nine months or more before anyone receives a distribution.

Would one of your beneficiaries be likely to need money sooner than the others? If so, you may want to make them the beneficiary of a life-insurance policy for part or all of their inheritance (assuming you have a life-insurance policy as part of your assets).

Is there likely to be a squabble over the estate by a disgruntled family member? This can tie things up for a long time. Life insurance, on the other hand, is pretty much incontestable and not subject to the same kind of claims that can be brought against an estate.

The insurance company simply doesn't care if Uncle Louis feels he's owed money and has an IOU scrawled on a cocktail napkin. If it isn't on file on their beneficiary form at the home office, it doesn't exist, period, the end.

Another convenient feature of life insurance is that it is *private*. An estate and all its details are a public record and easily accessible once it is filed. Not so with life insurance. Just try calling an insurance company for information if you are not the owner or beneficiary. It will be a very short conversation. So, is there some cause, institution or individual you'd like to leave money to and not have anyone know who it is or how much?

If you're planning on setting up a living trust, life insurance can also be a useful asset. When you put the insurance in, the cash value of the policy is the relevant number for any tax or fee. But the death benefit is likely to be much higher, even on a very old policy. So, this balloons the value of the trust when you pass on.

Generally, when we are talking about life insurance and its uses, we are thinking about old policies that you've had for years, not buying a new policy in most cases. Even if you have no need for the life insurance in any of the above circumstances, you may want to hold on to a policy purely for investment reasons. When you factor in all the loads, expenses and mortality cost you've paid over the years, they may not be showing a particularly good investment return overall. But that isn't the relevant question. The question is: "How do they work *now* if you keep the policy another year and probably pay another premium?"

To calculate the answer, you need your most recent annual statement from the insurance company. This will usually show the current year's, as well as last year's, cash value. Subtract last year's cash value from the current year's value, and that will give you your gross return in dollars. Now subtract any premium you paid to get the net growth number. Finally, divide that number by the previous year's cash value, and that will give you a percent return for the year. You may be surprised at your return.

Plus, it's not currently taxable and never taxable if paid out as a death benefit. Not at all a bad component of your overall investment plan, especially since it has no market risk. So, you can hold the asset for its investment value even if you have no need for the death benefit. Then, perhaps a few years down the road, circumstances might change and you'll have need for the policy in one of the special circumstances we were discussing above.

A final thought on legacy planning when you are leaving assets to your married children. Divorce is common and not just for younger people. In fact, the most rapidly increasing divorce rate is for people over age sixty. State laws vary a great deal but in most states, it is fairly difficult to keep inherited assets out of the divorce settlement unless they are segregated in a trust.

Do you want to leave some of your money to your children? How would you want your legacy handled in the event of a divorce? If you would like your money to stay with your offspring, you need to work this into your legacy planning. Make it clear to your attorney when you're updating your will.

The key is, *you* should be the bad one who disinherited your son-in-law by leaving the money for your daughter in a trust. When he finds out, you'll be gone and can afford to take one for the team. Don't leave your children to deal with it.

Ironically, when one married partner inherits and then takes the necessary steps to keep the assets separate, that action by itself can be the start of trouble in the marriage. Don't put your children in that awkward spot when you can easily take care of it in your estate plan.

Finally, don't forget your pets! Put some serious thought into what you want to have happen when you're gone. Don't assume your son or daughter will "of course" take Fluffy in unless you've talked about it and can see that it would be a good working arrangement for both Fluffy and your offspring.

If you don't have an appropriate family member or friend who can deal with your pet, you might want to make some arrangements with a local animal-protection group so they can step in and help. In your will you can give them the legal authority to do that. I always think it's best to sweeten the deal with a legacy donation, so they can put their heart into it.

Of course, someone might snicker because you left $20,000 to your cat, but so what? It's your money, and you can do what you want with it. Besides, you'll be in the Elysian Fields listening to Mozart or Bill Evans rather than snide snickers. And Fluffy will very much appreciate you making sure she isn't headed for a shelter when the time comes.

But if you do want to ensure privacy for such a bequest, there's an easy way to do that. Simply leave Fluffy's money to your donor-advised fund. (See chapter 8—if you don't already have one, they can be quick and easy to set up.) This request in your will is clearly a charitable bequest, and no one will give it a second thought. Any details about your DAF and what it does with the money are totally private and can't be accessed by anyone.

At the same time as you do this, simply specify to the DAF that at your death you would like them to make grants of a certain dollar amount to a charity or charities that you have set something up with to care for your pet. (These charities must be 501(c)(3) organizations and most animal-protection groups are.) Let the charity know you've left them funds in your estate and where they will come from.

Slick, classy and totally private.

Chapter Eleven: The Annual Review

The annual review is easy to ignore or put off. Especially when things are going well. The stock market is up and your cash flow is ideal so why take the time and effort to sit down with your planner and review everything? Well, mostly it's because we want to be sure there hasn't been some change we need to adjust for.

The annual review will always cover a host of things, and you never know what will turn out to be important. There's a list of routine items that need to be checked each year, even though the answers are almost always "no change." Here's a sample:

1. *Have you changed banks?*

2. *Any large expenses on the horizon?*

3. *Same employer?*

4. *Do any of your beneficiary arrangements need to be changed?*

5. *Any changes to your legacy plans?*

6. *Any significant changes in your financial circumstances?*

7. *Have there been any changes to your expenses?*

Any one of these items can be significant, so we have to take the time to ask.

For your investment portfolio, your planner also needs to review the following:

1. *Your current asset mix*

2. *Your volatility as a result of the asset mix*

3. *Any changes in your time horizon*

4. *The fees and expenses you are paying*

5. *The investment objective for the portfolio*

6. *Your investment results*

In reviewing your investment results, you need to keep a few guidelines in mind. Usually you are looking at the most recent calendar year or perhaps the trailing twelve months if you are well into the current year. The numbers, by themselves, are not the whole story.

Every style or type of investing goes in and out of favor. There are several studies on this effect but to cite just one, they prepared a list of the top-quartile performers for a ten-year period—these are the people you would want managing your money. Then they dug into the year-by-year results to see what percentage of these same managers *underperformed for a three-year period during that ten years.*

The results were astonishing. Virtually all—95%—of the managers looked pretty bad over some three-year time frame.* We already know, with the benefit of hindsight, that all of these managers were winners at the end of ten years.

Source: Davis Advisors. One hundred and fifty managers from eVestment Alliance's large cap universe whose ten-year gross of fees average annualized performance ranked in the top quartile from January 1, 2003 to December 31, 2012.

But within the ten years, most of them looked like they had lost their touch for a while.

Styles go in and out of favor, but good managers don't change their investment style just because the market isn't appreciating their approach at the moment. They just stick to their knitting.

This phenomenon has probably been observed ever since we've had markets. It doesn't fool investors who take the long view. But many new investors, juiced up on emotion and hard wired to fail at investing anyway, fall into this trap over and over again.

This "hard wired to fail" comment probably needs some explanation. Scientists have observed that, for all of our civilized nature, we still have some Neanderthal reactions at an instinctive level. Mental heuristics that kept our hunter-gatherer ancestors alive work very poorly with the stock market.

When we are in an unfamiliar or uncertain situation, our bodies produce a stress hormone called cortisol that pushes us to seek safety and familiarity. A recent study found that bond traders all have elevated levels of cortisol when they are in difficult trading environments, *and this affects their trading decisions*. New SLLS investors are probably gushing the stuff.[*]

Much of the work in this area for investments comes under the broad heading of "behavioral investing," which attempts to explain why smart people frequently make such bad investment decisions. Essentially, we fall victim to one

---

[*] *"From Molecule to Market: Steroid Hormones and Financial Risk-Taking" by John M. Coates, Mark Gurnell and Zoltan Sarnyai. Jan 27, 2010.*

or more of the thinking biases. The Dunning-Kruger effect (overconfidence), Herd Behavior, Availability Bias, the Halo Effect and Recency Bias all play a role in our investment decisions. In essence, we're trying to run new software on 150,000-year-old hardware. A Swiss study concluded that 45% of our decisions are based on genetics rather than reasoned thought.[*]

Here's how this usually plays out. When you invested your SLLS last year you had rosy expectations based on all the great managers you were using. Now, at your annual review, something is obviously wrong with Manager B. Those primitive emotions come alive and start sending out a danger warning. Let's walk through it.

Manager B is underperforming. But your financial advisor comforts you and explains that it's nothing to worry about. You understand and realize you've got to allow for this. Another year goes by, and you're doing your second annual review, and Manager B is still underperforming and might have gotten even worse in terms of relative results.

Now you're very unhappy and concerned. After all, it's been *two years*, and that's a long time. But your advisor is urging you to stick to the plan, and you say okay, but in the back of your mind, you're thinking you'll give this one more year to right itself.

Now comes your third annual review, and, of course, nothing looks any better. It's been three years! You can't put up with this anymore and insist that the manager be changed.

---

[*] *"The Genetics of Investment Biases" by Henrik Cronqvist and Stephan Siegel. August 20, 2013.*

After all, you've been more than patient. This manager has obviously lost their touch and can't manage money anymore. So, whom do you and your advisor replace the loser with? *Clearly someone who has a great record over the last 3–5 years.*

And what happens? The manager you just fired may well now go on a tear and have great returns over the next seven years or so. Of course, you won't know this because no one ever follows up to see how that manager is doing. And your new manager with the hot record? You guessed it. They could well go into their own three-year slump.

It's very much like being in a back-up on the expressway. You notice the lane to your right is moving much faster, so you risk a fender and slip into that lane. You know the story; the lane you were just in takes off and your new lane is stopped dead.

This scenario plays out time and time again. What's really sad is that too many investment advisors are no better. Rather than defend the manager who's going through a rough patch, it's much easier to capitulate and show they are looking out for your interests by firing this manager.

Which is why many "investment committees" who oversee trusts, pensions or your 401(k) options have poor results. They follow the same pattern as our amateur investor. Surely, they have the responsibility of only keeping good managers. "Good" is defined in their minds as someone who never has a period of being out of favor. That's what made Bernie Madoff so popular; he always got a steady 9% return in all markets…right up until they put the handcuffs on.

This same story shows up when we look at a mutual fund's returns over ten years versus the average investors in the same fund. The fund does well, but the investors earn far less because they keep jumping in and out. In a 2013 Lipper/Dalbar study, the spread was especially large. The fund earned 8.6% over the ten years, while their average investor only got 4.3%.[*]

So, when you look at returns, **don't expect every fund or SMA in your portfolio to do well every year**. Be prepared to stick with a manager unless there has been some fundamental change or key personnel turnover. Never fire a manage solely because their returns are off—even for three years.

Changing managers or funds should only be considered in a few circumstances:

- *Your investment objective has changed and the fund no longer fits.*

- *Key personnel or other changes at the fund have occurred and are unfavorable.*

- *A new or different fund appears to be a better fit for your objective for reasons other than investment results.*

Keep in mind—strange as it may seem—investment results are potentially the worst possible way to select or monitor investment funds. Be wary of an investment advisor that leads with the trailing return as a reason for including a fund or SMA in the portfolio. Instead, the focus should be

---

[*] *Source:* Quantitative Analysis of Investor Behavior *by Dalbar, Inc. (March 2013) and Lipper. Dalbar computed the "average stock fund investor return" by using industry cash flow reports from the Investment Company Institute. All Dalbar returns were computed using the S&P 500® Index.*

on what *investment characteristics* a manager brings to the table and why you need them.

The biggest reason for looking at returns during the annual review is to see how your plan is working and if you are on target. By monitoring each year—now that we know what one more year's actual results were—you can stay on track by making adjustments.

A final reason for annual reviews is to let your planner get to know you better and for you to get more comfortable with them. Typically, it takes the exposure of working together for several years to get a great working relationship. But it will be well worth the effort.

Conclusion

On pretty much every topic covered here, about 75% is left out. Subjects dealt with in a couple paragraphs could be whole books in themselves. And even if you had the patience to read a dozen books on the subject, and are a quick study, that still wouldn't mean you should go it alone. You can only learn so much from books. What is critically needed is *experience*, and you probably don't have the time for that.

Consider buying that experience by hiring a seasoned financial planner. If you've just come into a sudden large lump sum, there is no reason to gamble. It's a classic small mistake/big mistake scenario. If you pay a planner a 1% fee for five years and that turns out to be unnecessary, you've made a 5% mistake. But if you go it alone and blunder, it can easily turn into a big mistake that costs a whole lot more.

If that makes sense to you, this book has succeeded.

Index

Appendix: Questions to Ask a Potential Financial Planner

Before meeting with a potential financial planner, do check the FINRA web page to see when they got licensed and if there are any customer complaints that are disclosed.

Go to finra.org, then look for "broker check"—it's usually on the first page and clearly marked. For "firm name" be sure to use the broker dealer name, not the local trade name.

When you have a preliminary meeting with a potential advisor, you may want to let the meeting proceed naturally for fifteen minutes or so and then begin to work in your questions. That way, a few of the questions may have already been answered. Also, some of these questions may be covered in the firm's brochure or web page, and you can just request any clarification you need.

In any case, here are a few questions you definitely want to have answers to before choosing a planner to work with.

1. What is your investment philosophy?

What you're looking for here is someone who has a clear idea of what their philosophy is and can articulate it. Are they focused primarily on active management or indexes?

A follow-up question might be "How do you prepare for bear markets?" If their answer is any variation of

"We see them coming and move everything to T-bills" flee as soon as possible without being too rude.

2. How do you put together a financial plan? What's the procedure?

If their answer is anything along the lines of "We give you forty pages of questions for you to fill out at home and mail back to us" that is not good. The questions and your responses should be discussed and clarified as you go. Ideally, you'll meet with the planner in person to have a dialogue. The planner needs to understand you and your concerns. Some planners may have you meet with an associate or staff member for the data gathering. I don't like that approach as I find the more time I spend getting to know a new client, the better. If the planner uses a staff member to gather information, it is probably a sign that they are working with a larger number of clients.

3. How many clients do you (not the firm) work with? Is there a target number where you won't take any more?

This will tell you a lot about what kind of personal attention you will be receiving.

The lower the number, the better for you. I feel as you move up from one hundred clients there needs to be more staff involvement and appointments are more tightly scheduled. In my case, for example, I like to do an "internal review" for every client once a year, usually six months after the normal annual review. This is where I have a meeting with myself about your account to see if there is anything that needs to be looked at. These "meetings" take

134

between fifteen minutes and three hours and have become essential in my mind. When it's just me, alone in my office mulling over the details of a plan, I frequently come up with ideas to explore and think about. But it also adds to the time-per-client equation and reduces the number of clients I can work with.

4. Could you give me a brief profile of what your client base is like in terms of age, profession and account size? Do you have a specialty?

Since you are looking for someone with expertise with income or retirement portfolios, you can draw your own conclusions from their answer. Also, if they have a specialty, such as business owners, doctors or professional athletes, and that is not what you are, you may wonder if you'll be a less important client in their eyes.

5. How often would we meet for reviews?

Annual reviews are the most common, with other meetings as needed. The only reason for asking is just to make sure you are both on the same page here. If the planner doesn't seem to be concerned about annual reviews, that's a red flag.

6. How accessible are you for questions after the plan is in place? Would I normally be talking with you or a staff person?

There is no wrong answer here, but the planner should deliver on whatever is promised. Over the years, I've taken over more accounts from other planners for this reason than any other.

7. What are your fees?

The fee schedule may well be on the planner's website or brochure, but you should clarify some details. Is the planner fee only, or do they also get commissions? If the planner is fee only, are they with a reputable broker dealer? In most cases the broker dealer's name will not be familiar—which is okay—but make at least a quick Google search. If the firm is very small, with fewer than a hundred employees, for example, do a little extra research before signing up. Many planners charge a separate fee for the initial plan.

Note one question NOT to ask: "Can you provide references?"

The most larcenous, corrupt, dishonest planner in the country can readily provide three references. Bernie Madoff had great references. When I'm asked this question, I always say: "No, I respect my clients' privacy. If you were my client, would you want me to give your name out so some stranger could call to ask you a bunch of questions?"

Even if you did, what possible good could it do? This person you called might only be a simple shill. How would you know? It's all pointless and a waste of time.